THE LONGEST DATE

Cindy Chupack has won three Golden Globes and two Emmys for her work as a writer/producer of HBO's *Sex and the City* and ABC's *Modern Family*. Several episodes she penned were individually nominated for Writers Guild and Emmy awards. Chupack's other TV credits include *Everybody Loves Raymond*, *Coach*, and the hour-long romantic comedy anthology series she created for NBC, *Love Bites* (which can be viewed on Hulu .com). She has written about dating and relationships for many publications and had her own column in *Glamour* and *O, The Oprah Magazine*. She now lives in Los Angeles with her husband, her St. Bernard, and . . . you'll just have to read the book.

The
Longest
Date

~~~~~~~~~~~~~~~~~~~~

Life as a Wife

Cindy Chupack

Penguin Books

PENGUIN BOOKS
Published by the Penguin Group
Penguin Group (USA) LLC
375 Hudson Street
New York, New York 10014

USA | Canada | UK | Ireland | Australia | New Zealand | India | South Africa | China
penguin.com
A Penguin Random House Company

First published in the United States of America by Viking Penguin,
a member of Penguin Group (USA) LLC, 2014
Published in Penguin Books 2014

THE LIBRARY OF CONGRESS HAS CATALOGED
THE HARDCOVER EDITION AS FOLLOWS:
. Chupack, Cindy.
The longest date : life as a wife / Cindy Chupack.
pages cm
ISBN 978-0-670-02553-4 (hc.)
ISBN 978-0-14-312615-7 (pbk.)
1. Marriage—Humor. 2. Wives—Humor. 3. Man-woman relationships—Humor.
I. Title.
PN6231.M3.C46 2014
306.81'0207—dc23   2013036805

Printed in the United States of America
1 3 5 7 9 10 8 6 4 2

For Ian, who not only made this book possible,
he made it a love story.

Contents

Contents

Contents

The
Longest
Date

Introduction

I've always been a romantic. When I was single, I slept only with men I believed I could marry.

That would be admirable except for one detail: I slept with a lot of men.

A lot a lot.

I'm not going to tell you the exact number because my parents might read this book, and they certainly don't need to know the tally.

And also, I don't know it.

Don't judge me.

I was single for a long time.

Alcohol was often involved.

I didn't keep a guest book by my bed, so, yes, some names were lost along the way.

The point is not my incomplete sexual history, okay? It's the more troublesome issue that every time there was a man inside of me, there was also a voice inside of me saying *This might be the man I marry!*

Clearly, I knew nothing about the reality of marriage. Or hormones.

I'm not sure which was more dangerous—my casual attitude toward sex or my delusions of love—but one led to the other in a decade-long binge of salty and sweet, horny and hopeful.

Finally, after enough relationship wreckage to fill a book (*The Between Boyfriends Book*), two magazine columns, and five seasons of *Sex and the City*, at the age of thirty-eight I found a guy I absolutely did not want to marry, and, of course, he's the guy I wound up marrying.

I'm not saying I settled. I'm saying I met a wildly attractive, interesting, smart, funny guy who had so many red flags—many of which he voluntarily and repeatedly waved in my face—that I told my coworkers at *Sex and the City*, "Do not let me fall for this one," and that's when, they say, they knew that I would do precisely that.

We'd all seen the romantic comedies; we drank the Kool-Aid. Hell, we were *making* the Kool-Aid. So it was hilariously predicatable that, like every other rom-com heroine, I found my happy ending when I least expected it, music up, wedding montage, cue credits!

Or not.

Turns out "happily ever after" is the epitome of lazy writing.

Maybe fictional characters live happily ever after, but for the nonfictional rest of us, the story continues with a lot more complexity, and in a way, marriage winds up being the longest date ever.

And however much we think we know how to do dating, on this date, you can't decide not to see him again because you're tired of hearing him talk about cheese. For example.

You have to try to work things out, or at least appear to try, and as it turns out, I was completely unprepared for this job.

I got married at forty (despite my lobbying efforts to move the wedding up a month so I would still be thirty-nine). I remember complaining to friends that, because of my age, my husband and I would have to start trying to have kids right away. I sincerely wished we were younger—that we had five years to be just a couple.

And I got my wish. We didn't become magically younger, but we did get five years to ourselves, thanks to the myriad problems we encountered trying to have a child.

So what did I learn in those five years? And how can I help you prepare for that thing about your spouse that you must somehow embrace because he's your spouse? (Wanna hear about cheese?) The fertility problems you might face because it took two decades to find a guy to face them with? Disagreements about pets, space, houseguests (I think I'm adverse to them because I still secretly feel my husband is one), couples therapy, entertaining together, cleanliness, vows (every anniversary we rewrite ours and have the option to sign up for another year—so far so good), and sex? What about married sex?

Oh yes, I am an authority on sex. In fact, I was a sex columnist for *O, The Oprah Magazine* while we were going through IVF treatments, and I finally gave up my column because sex had become so fraught for me, so synonymous with failure, that I could no longer in good conscience advise women on how to "spice up their sex lives" with porn and lingerie. I felt like a fucking fraud, literally and figuratively.

So, in this book, I wanted to tell the honest, horrible, hysterical truth about the early years of marriage. I certainly could have used some preparation, or at least some commiseration.

I also noticed a lack of humor and hope in most of what's been written about infertility. Women I know—and even women I don't know—encouraged me to fill this void when they responded so enthusiastically to the first piece I ever published about the trying nature of trying: "We're Having a Maybe!" (which is now a chapter of this book).

The one thing my husband, Ian, and I learned from this experience is, never say never. In fact, as I began writing this book, we found ourselves in a craft store buying construction paper for the scrapbook we'd been advised to make for prospective birth mothers. Yes, we now had to market ourselves as parents.

I never thought I would be in that position—not the adopting part (we'd always been open to adoption) but construction paper? Really? But our adoption lawyer said our scrapbook should look homemade, so we spent a weekend gluing photos of ourselves (with friends, with family, on holidays, on vacation) onto Easter egg–colored construction paper, which we hole punched and bound with ribbons.

And as we were doing this, as we were making this little Book of Us, I realized we had, somehow, amid the chaos and confusion of cohabitation, built a lovely life together. There we were, page after pastel page, two people (and one St. Bernard I didn't think I wanted) who had shared five years of adventures (good and bad, large and small) that had strengthened our bond as a couple.

So I'm grateful for those five years, hard earned as they were, and although "happily ever after" still strikes me as the romantic equivalent of the Rapture (sure, it might happen, but let's not spend our lives waiting for it), I am writing this book for every woman who ever was or will be blindsided by the reality of marriage: to validate and celebrate life as a wife.

When Cindy Met Ian

When I met Ian, I was somewhere between a slump and a decision.

I hadn't had sex in nine months, which seemed dangerously close to a year. And although I'd racked up a decent (however inexact) number of lovers in the past, not having sex for a year when you're single feels like it could easily become two years, then three, and before you know it, the only relationships you care about are in *Us Weekly*, and your entire wardrobe is velour.

Part of me thought I should just have sex with someone, anyone, to end my slump before the year was up, but I wasn't sure if that would make me feel empowered or desperate.

The other part of me felt that you don't become a vegetarian for nine months and then start eating meat again by buying a random hot dog on the street. Maybe I should wait for a steak, a filet mignon, something delicious, something I might love, since I'd waited so long already.

Of course, calling the sexual blackout I'd experienced

"waiting" was romantic semantics at their best. But the way I figured it, I'd been celibate for nine months whether I intended it or not. And nine months of waiting to find a man who was worthy of sharing my bed sounded a hell of a lot better than nine months of failing to find a guy who even wanted to kiss me.

By calling it "waiting," I felt as if I was reclaiming control of my romantic destiny. As if I'd ever controlled it in the first place. As if anyone could control anything having to do with love. All I could really control was whether I would call my current predicament a slump or a decision, so I went with decision. I *decided* since I'd *waited* almost a year already (see how this works?), I would not sleep with a man unless I was in love. Preferably with him.

It was basically an attitude shift, but an exciting one, because as soon as I realized/decided that I was no longer in a slump, I felt much happier. I started going out more, saying yes more often. Concert on a weeknight? Why not?

That's how I found myself at a Dave Matthews concert in Central Park with my friend Mark. Mark had tickets not only to the concert, but to the VIP reception beforehand. I remember scanning the VIP tent and thinking *How will I meet a man I might date if it looks like I'm on a date with Mark, who doesn't want to date me?* And then, *Why* doesn't *Mark want to date me?*

I'd known Mark for years. He was handsome and smart, and nobody could make me laugh like he did. We got along great, we were each other's default date to weddings, but he'd only ever wanted to be friends. And as much as I would have preferred to believe Mark was gay, he wasn't. I just wasn't The One for him, and he wasn't the type to sleep with random hot dogs from the street, which is why I thought he might be gay, because most straight guys don't care where they get their meat, but Mark had integrity and valued our friendship, blah blah blah.

In the romantic comedy version of this story, I would marry Mark, the one who was there all along. But I did not.

I also did not marry someone I met in the VIP tent. In fact, as the night wore on, I felt more like a Virtually Invisible Person than a Very Important one. Nobody seemed the least bit interested in me. Or rather, nobody interested me in the least (to reinvoke romantic semantics).

But after the concert (which was a great concert, despite my realization that I would never date Mark or anyone else I might meet while with Mark), Mark and I decided to catch the end of a Moth storytelling event at The Players, a private club in Gramercy Park.

And it was there, at The Players, that I met a true player, Ian.

He'd come with a date, I learned later, but he left with me.

That's kind of sexy if you're me. Not so much if you were his date.

If you are reading this, Ian's date of that night, I owe you an apology. Not for that night—you left early because you had work to do, and with a guy like Ian, you must have known that was the equivalent of a green light. But I owe you an apology because, years later, when we ran into you outside of Canal Jeans in SoHo and Ian introduced us, I was less than attentive, having met one too many beautiful women Ian "used to know." I think I made a phone call instead of talking to you, and for that I am deeply sorry. If it helps, when I am annoyed with Ian, I think of you as the one who got away.

Not the one whom Ian let get away.

The one who got away *from a life with Ian*.

By the end of this book, I hope you and everyone else reading this will understand how, at times, a wife might envy the one who got away and still be extremely happy she's the one who did not.

Now, in New York, it's perfectly normal to do one amazing thing (like see a Dave Matthews concert in Central Park) and then continue on to another amazing thing (like a Moth event, where people get onstage and share their true, well-crafted stories), as opposed to in Los Angeles, where you have to factor in traffic and a general lack of interest in leaving the house in order to see something mildly entertaining, let alone potentially amazing.

I used to go to Moth events in New York just to sit in the audience, but sometimes I also got onstage to tell stories, so I always knew a lot of people there, and one of those people introduced me to a guy who had won the last "story slam."

Story slams are the Moth's rowdier, open-mic storytelling shows that are held in the East Village (as opposed to the main-stage curated events that I had done in the past, like the one that night at The Players). This might seem like a random detail, but I bring it up because although I was "main stage" and Ian was "open mic," it was probably the other way around, dating-wise.

I remember thinking Ian was handsome, but I guess I was still scarred from the VIP tent, because after the show, when Mark wanted to stay and socialize, I just wanted to go home. It was late for a weeknight, I was tired, and I wasn't on a date with Mark, so I left.

Ian happened to be leaving at the same time. Only later did he admit this was not a coincidence, that he left because he saw me walk out. (Like I said, he was a player.) He struck up a conversation on the sidewalk, and we talked about storytelling and our jobs, and he said we should go out for a drink, and I agreed and started to give him my number, and he grinned a devilish grin and said, "I meant *now*."

He was inviting me out for a drink *now*.

Suddenly I was on a date on a night when I had come to terms with the fact that I was not.

Except, *was* it a date? It seemed like a date. We met, he asked me out for a drink. The fact that the date started immediately, instead of two weeks later, after I'd spent fourteen days wondering if he would call, didn't really matter, did it?

Maybe it did. Maybe I was being picked up. On the street. Like a random hot dog.

In any case, it was happening. We went to a bar that was a block away, because in New York you are always a block away from a bar; that's another reason why it's such a great city. And at the bar we talked and drank, and laughed and drank, and drank some more, and then at some point Ian said he was a good poet, and I said I was, too, having written a lot of poetry in my day. But then I realized I was completely out-leagued, because Ian said he could improvise a poem on any topic I gave him. So I gave him "a kiss," and he proceeded to rap/recite a long, seductive, impromptu poem extolling the virtues of a kiss, which, of course, made me want to kiss him, and by the end of the poem we were kissing (me on a bar stool, Ian standing), and it was sexy and magical until I noticed the bartender rolling his eyes.

That's when it occurred to me that maybe this wasn't the first time Ian had romanced women with poetry. Maybe it wasn't even the first time he'd done it at this bar. It also occurred to me that really, I didn't give a shit.

We decided to go to my apartment, because it was closer than Ian's. We were going to *someone's* apartment, that much was clear. I remember warning Ian that my place was nice (I think I was afraid it would be intimidating or something), and he said, "What the hell? Mine's nice, too!" and then we started to walk the short walk to my street. Well, *I* started to walk. Ian was waving down a cab, once again proving that his idea of immediate gratification was much more immediate than mine.

We kissed in the cab, we kissed on my steps, we made out against the wall in my foyer, and eventually we fell into my bed and ended my slump—twice.

And the next morning I woke up in Ian's arms and said, "Wow, I haven't done that in a while . . ." and then I realized it was *because I was supposed to be in love with the guy*!

I had fallen off the wagon, and not with a great guy, but with a bad boy!

I'd have to keep looking. I would continue to sleep with Ian (because—who am I kidding?—I'm not a vegetarian) but I would keep seeking the guy I was going to marry; Ian was not that guy. He told me he wasn't that guy. He said he didn't want a relationship, that he would break my heart, that he was trouble.

And it was all a big, fat lie. Ian was the one who decided we should be exclusive. He asked me out for Halloween, and when I told him I had a friend in town, and that the next night my friend would still be in town, Ian realized my friend was a guy (like I said, I was still looking!) and said, "Have a nice time, whore!" and that's when I knew Ian cared about me.

Ian was the first one to say "I love you," which came as a shock to both of us. It was after a dinner party we'd thrown together a few months after we'd met (yes, the guy who didn't want to be in a relationship decided we should introduce our friends), and afterward, as we were cleaning up, I saw a mouse run under my couch. Ian tried to coax it out (which worked—it came out and ran directly into the kitchen *between my feet* to get to another room, the first sign that having a man around to take care of things like mice was not necessarily going to take care of things like mice), but that was so hilarious-slash-upsetting that we left my apartment in the care of the mouse and went out for a drink with two of Ian's friends, and as they were laughing at the story, Ian looked at me and said he loved me. They didn't hear him, but who says "I love you" for the first time with other people at the table? Ian did. And it was twice as heart pounding because it was so completely unexpected.

Ian was the one who decided to take the California bar exam so he could be where my career was.

Ian was the one, the day after taking the California bar exam, who said he was going surfing, then surprised me on the beach near my house at sunset to propose, riding a white horse, dressed as a knight. I know that sounds potentially corny, but he pulled it off . . . rented armor, rented horse, and all. In fact, he told me later that the horse had started galloping when he first got on, and his rented helmet closed, obscuring his vision, so all he saw was "dog, sand, ocean, sand." And then when he finally slowed down and got to me, his foot had slipped out of the stirrup and he couldn't get the faux armor foot covering back into the stirrup in order to get off the horse and propose. When I saw what was going on, I asked if he needed help, and he said, "No, this is something I need to do myself." And then a few seconds later, he conceded, "Yes, I need help." So he rescued me, just like in the fairy tales, but I had to help him get off his high horse. And then the horse—who had once appeared on *Will & Grace*, because in Los Angeles even animals have credits—had to go back to Hollywood, so I got to walk hand in hand with my fiancé/knight-in-shining-rented-armor back to the beach house where I had lived for so long alone, and as neighbors and passersby stopped and stared, I thought, a little smugly, *They said it wouldn't happen.*

Ian was the one who wanted to have kids right away.

Ian was The One.

And the rest is romantic semantics. The sweet version of this story is that I had decided that the next guy I slept with would be someone I loved, and he turned out to be precisely that. The salty version is that I did not have the willpower (or sobriety) to wait until I was in love to sleep with someone, but I fell in love with the guy I didn't wait to sleep with.

Get This

I'm finally getting married!"

That's what I kept telling people.

I didn't say I was finally getting married *again*, because bringing up a first marriage during the planning of a second seemed to be a major buzzkill for everyone involved, especially me. I suppose this is because it reminds the bride and groom, at a time when their biggest worry should be buttercream versus spun sugar, that these partnerships don't always work out. That love does not always conquer all. And I didn't want to hang that particular cloud over Ian, because this was his first wedding (a term I didn't like for him either, because it implied he might have a second). So we tried not to talk about first or second anythings until our first meeting with the rabbi.

Ian called our rabbi "the hot rabbi," because she was young and hip and, okay, let's just say it: hot. I didn't mind him calling her hot. In fact, I found it reassuring, because it was a clear sign, exactly when I needed one, that Ian was not gay. The one wedding detail I was certain about was this: *I did not want to publicly declare my love for someone in front of my closest friends and family only to have that someone, two years later, realize he might be gay.* Again.

Yes, okay, yes. That's what happened to me the first time around, a little over ten years earlier, and that's what I told the hot rabbi when she asked if either of us had been married before.

The hot rabbi blinked, then nodded. Like I said, she was hip. She lived in New York. What woman today doesn't have a guy-who-turned-out-to-be-gay story? Admittedly, it's a smaller, somewhat sadder subset that has a husband-who-turned-out-to-be-gay story, but the point is the hot rabbi was appropriately not shocked. She said she didn't need to know all of the details, although she was happy to listen if I needed to talk.

But I didn't need to talk about that particular topic. I have talked about it so much that the story is on Audible.com (seriously). We were both in our twenties. The divorce was amicable. We labeled index cards with our meager belongings and divided them up. We shared a cat for a while. It stung me a bit when I realized my ex was going to have a husband and kids before I did. I think it stung him a bit when he realized I was getting paid more to write sitcoms than he was getting paid to save lives. So we gave each other space to have—or have not—without judgment.

The hot rabbi did ask if my ex-husband was Jewish. This seemed like a moot point to me, but I told her, Yes, he was Jewish. She nodded again and made a note.

I remember how happy my parents had been that I was

marrying a Jewish doctor. It was like winning the Jewish lottery, until he turned out to be gay. After that, my parents cared less about my boyfriends' religion than their ability to name at least three pro ballplayers. Therefore, it was nice, but not essential, that Ian turned out to be Jewish as well.

Ian was a tattooed lawyer/poet/chef who had learned French while living in Vietnam, sold rare books in Paris, and interned in The Hague, where he helped draft the Milošević indictment. The fact that he was Jewish was the least remarkable thing about him.

In the spirit of full disclosure, Ian told the hot rabbi that his mother had converted to Judaism before he was born, but she might now consider herself more of a Buddhist, and while we were on the subject of the gays, she was also a late-in-life lesbian who had recently married a woman. The hot rabbi made another note, then mused that it was perhaps fitting that our wedding was taking place during New York's gay pride weekend.

This fact, I have to admit, had somehow eluded me. As I started contemplating the irony of this, and wondering which of our carefully laid plans might be interrupted by the parade route, Ian helpfully went on to explain that his dad was Jewish, and although his dad died when Ian was young, Ian still considered himself a Jew, and wanted a Jewish wedding, so here we were.

Ian and the hot rabbi smiled at me. I smiled back, pretending to have been paying attention. Then the hot rabbi had this question for me: "Did you ever get a get?"

I had heard of a get. I knew it was some kind of Jewish divorce certificate, but it felt like Number 1,764 on my list of priorities when my marriage ended—slightly less pressing than figuring out what to do with all of our wedding photos, and about as exciting as informing my credit card companies that I needed to change my name back.

Plus, I had never been that religious. I hadn't even had a bat mitzvah, because my sister had warned me, "If you're doing it for the presents, that's the wrong reason." Then, when the time came, she did have a bat mitzvah and raked it in, which, she admitted as an adult, had been her plan all along.

Whatever. I'm over it. But since my thirteen-year-old self hadn't gotten the gifts, the party, or much of a Jewish identity, my twenty-seven-year-old self had been in no rush to get a Jewish divorce certificate. Our non-Jewish divorce had been complicated enough, especially since I was attempting to fill out the forms myself with the help of a do-your-own-divorce book and a gay production assistant from the show where I was working.

I mention the gay production assistant not only because he was very helpful, but also because at that time in my life—when my marriage was ending for the most irreconcilable of differences—it seemed as if everyone in the world was gay. It wasn't just my husband: two of his groomsmen came out after our wedding, as did, in a very unexpected twist, one of my bridesmaids. Looking back, I'm not sure if it was a wedding party or a White Party.

I was tinkering with stand-up comedy then, and onstage

my routines involved only subjects like why a clerk at the 99 Cents store would shout, "Price check!" Offstage, however, I would talk to my friend Rob, a fellow aspiring stand-up, about everything else. Rob was a big guy with big glasses and a big personality. He was also the first person who tried to make me laugh about the fact that my husband had realized he was gay. Rob was endlessly fascinated and amused by my story, and asked me a lot of questions like: What were the signs? Has he told his family yet? How did he tell you?

A year later, Rob came out. He also lost about half of his body weight, since he wasn't hiding anymore, and it became clear to me that in Rob's eyes (now in contacts), my husband was the hero of my story.

My story: every time I told it, someone came out to me. I was telling it at a Hollywood party to a cute guy I thought was flirting with me only to realize he was married—to a man. He explained that he had never even dated men until he met his husband while traveling abroad. Then I told that story to my friend who hosted the party, and he confessed that he considered himself bi, which he explained was difficult for any potential partner to comprehend. For example, he went on, how would *I* feel about dating him? When I realized his question was not rhetorical, I blushed and respectfully declined. Then I told *that* story to a male friend whom I knew was straight, and he also confessed he was thinking of dating men; then, months later, after coming out to his stunned Beverly Hills parents and getting a couple of gay relationships under his belt, so to speak, he decided he was actually more interested in women, and eventually he married a woman who had previously considered herself a lesbian. My feeling, at this point, when everyone's sexuality seemed to be in flux, was simply: Pick a side! I'm fine with it all! Just declare a major!

I was thinking about what a relief it was that I could finally tell my story without inadvertently encouraging anybody out of the closet when the hot rabbi announced that I should "get a get."

She explained that Ian and I did not technically need a get in order to get married, but without it, under Jewish law, our children would basically be considered bastards.

Wow. I was prepared for my children to be miracles of science, but bastards?

She clarified that this would only be a problem if those prospective children wanted to marry a nonbastard Jew or go to a Jewish school for nonbastards. (She didn't use those words exactly; she may have used the term "illegitimate," but that was the idea.) She also thought the process might be good closure for me.

Frankly, it sounded like anything *but* closure. It sounded like it would require reopening the lines of communication that my ex-husband and I had finally, and I would say mercifully, shut down, after trying for years to prove that we were the friends we kept saying we were. We were friends. We wished each other well. It was just easier, I think, to wish each other well from afar.

Also, we'd had a version of closure. At one point, when his

parents were having a hard time accepting the idea that their son was gay, that it was something he was born with, they cut him off financially. He was in med school at the time and strapped for cash, and the one thing he really wanted was to buy a house. So I decided to help him with the down payment by giving him back the extravagant emerald-cut engagement ring that he, out of guilt, had told me to keep. I had stored it in a safe-deposit box, not wanting to wear it but not quite ready to sell or reset it. I would occasionally visit my ring, visit my old married self, but even with nobody present to witness it, I was aware of how pathetic I looked sitting in a bank cubicle modeling my engagement ring. So when I had the opportunity to return it to its rightful owner in the spirit of forgiveness and friendship, I jumped at the chance. I said, "With this ring, will you not marry me?" And we had a little moment, and he bought a little house, and that was that.

Until now.

In order to get a get, I would need to get back in touch with my ex-husband and persuade him to go before a panel of three Orthodox holy men and officially "release me." The process is actually even more offensive than I am making it sound. The tradition is based on a completely sexist biblical verse (Deuteronomy 24:1), which states, in so many words: "A man takes a wife and possesses her. If she fails to please him because he finds something obnoxious about her, he writes her a bill of divorcement, hands it to her, and sends her away from his house."

First of all, I do not think my ex-husband found me

obnoxious. He might have wished I had a penis, but if anything, I was the one who had grounds for "sending him away from my house." However, with my wedding to Ian less than three months away and the hope of legitimate children on the horizon, I decided this was not the time to go Gloria Steinem on the Old Testament.

When I called my ex-husband in Los Angeles (I was living in New York at the time), he was surprised to hear from me, happy to learn I was getting married, and a little dubious about what I was asking him to do. I assured him I would pay the fee and do all the homework; his only responsibility would be to show up. We decided that although it was possible to get a get without being in the same place, we would try to get ours the next time I was in Los Angeles. He even suggested we have a "get-together" afterward so I could meet his kids. I started to like the idea of a get. It sounded like it might be good closure after all.

Our awkward reunion took place outside a barely marked industrial building that served as an office for the Orthodox rabbi whose name I had gotten through an online organization that facilitated gets. (Yes, there is such an organization, it's based in Brooklyn, and operators are standing by.) We made small talk while I pressed the buzzer (You look good. You, too. How are your parents? How's New York?) but it slowly became clear, as we ran out of chitchat, that nobody was responding to the buzzing. We called the rabbi's number, which was his home number, and he answered, and that's when we learned that there was confusion about the time and that we'd have to reschedule.

We explained that we couldn't reschedule. It had taken us over ten years to make this appointment.

The rabbi sighed and said he would try to locate two witnesses, and we should give him an hour.

That's how it came to pass that we had some time to kill, and my ex-husband said his partner and kids were nearby shopping, so maybe we should have our "get-together" now. It was too late for lunch and too early for dinner, which seemed appropriately symbolic of our relationship, but we found a faux–French café nearby that would take us.

It's not often a girl gets to sit down with the man she thought she would have kids with and the man he did have kids with (not to mention the kids), but the truth is, they were a pretty perfect family without me. I had met my ex-husband's partner at a Christmas party years earlier, and I liked him immediately. He was so handsome and kind and witty that I found it flattering to imagine he was the male version of me. They had since adopted two beautiful boys who looked as if they'd just crawled out of a Baby Gap ad. As I watched my ex-husband juggle juice boxes and crayons and children's menus, he smiled at me and warned: "Get ready."

I was getting ready. I was trying to make sure my kids wouldn't be bastards.

Finally the rabbi called and said he could see us. When we arrived, all of us, he explained the process might take another hour, so my ex-husband told his family he would call them when we were done.

The rabbi was old, and his two witnesses were even older. They sat on one side of a table and we sat on the other. We had to say our names in Hebrew, which already was a problem because mine was supposedly Ariel, but I was told in Sunday school that the female version of Ariel is Ariella. Feeling strongly that somebody should be the female version of me in this process, I went with Ariella. We also had to state that we had come freely without coercion, and then we watched in respectful silence as the rabbi, who was also officially a scribe, wrote our divorce document by hand, with pen and ink, in Hebrew.

After what seemed like an eternity, the document was only half finished. When my ex-husband left to feed the meter, the rabbi fixed me with a stare and asked the question that had clearly been bothering him since we arrived: "Who was that other man who came with you?" Since I wasn't sure what the official Orthodox stance was on homosexuality, I said it was my ex-husband's friend. "And whose children were those?" he asked. I didn't like where this was going. I asked if this would affect the get process, because we had been there a long time as it was. He assured me it would not, so I admitted that my ex-husband was gay, and that the other man was his partner, and those were their kids.

The two ancient witnesses looked at each other, which was the first and only indication that they spoke English.

"I think that's sick," the rabbi said flatly.

"It's not sick," I said. "They're very happy."

Then, in a terribly unoriginal attempt at a joke, the rabbi said, "Which one is the man?"

"They're both men," I said. "They're both very good men."

When my ex-husband came back into the room, I felt ill. I had flown cross-country, paid five hundred dollars, and dragged him to a warehouse so some Rent-a-Rabbi and his Manischewitz drinking buddies could sit in judgment of him. And the irony was, he was the practicing Jew, not I. I was fuming, wondering if we should forget the get, get out, get while the gettin' was good. I was composing an angry letter in my head, venting to the hot rabbi, praying this wasn't representative of my faith, when we were informed that our document was complete. Then we were asked to stand. And face each other. And then my ex-husband was asked to look into my eyes and repeat some phrases that meant basically "With this document, I release you."

And as we stood there, just as we had on our wedding day, he looked even more handsome. And grown-up. And happy. And I thought about why he had married me in the first place. Yes, he loved me, but also, he was probably afraid he would never be able to have a family if he didn't marry a woman. And now he had that family without having had to compromise any part of who he was. And I thought about what he had given me all of those years ago when he had unofficially released me. He gave me my single life back. And as much as I hated the heartbreak and longing, it became the basis of my writing career, which led me to a job on *Sex and the City*, which led me to New York, which led me to my tattooed lawyer/poet/chef.

And then I thought about how this tribunal, this ridiculous judgmental tribunal, was what my ex-husband faced every day, sometimes when he least expected it, sometimes from family, sometimes from within, and realized how hard it must have been for him to overcome that judgment in order to be honest with me and with himself. So, as he dropped the get into my open palms, which made it legally binding, I felt proud of him, and proud of us, for releasing each other to our proper destinies.

"I'm happy you're getting married," he said. "Now I can finally stop feeling guilty."

I told him he had no reason to feel guilty. But he said he couldn't help it.

Some things, I guess, we're just born with.

The Vows I Read at Our Wedding

A few years ago I was at a friend's wedding and I remember thinking, during the vows, what an important test it was: To be able to say, out loud, in front of your closest friends and family, why you were choosing to spend your life with this particular person. Why you loved this person. Why, of all the people in the world, *this* person. It really struck me . . . how enormous an admission that was, how I hoped I would be able to do that someday, and how I needed to break up with the guy I had brought to that wedding.

In the years that followed, that became my test of a relationship: could I answer those questions about whom I loved and why I loved him openly and honestly in front of all the people I cared about?

And here we are. And I can. And there is so much to say. It is such a relief to have so much to say (and not just to my therapist):

One thing I love about you, Ian, is that we have said most of these things to each other already. You never let a day go by when you don't tell me how much you love me. And this is, of course, after warning me early on that you didn't want to say "I love you" too often, because you felt it would lose its meaning. I love that you have no strength in your convictions when it comes to the limits of your love. You continue to surprise me, and yourself, I think, with your capacity to love and be loved.

I love that I can count on you completely. You always do more than you say you will. In fact, when I recently had a little health scare (which turned out to be nothing), your response was, "Not on my watch. Nothing is going to happen to you on *my* watch." And although you sometimes seem to have superpowers, I know you can't stop bad things from happening to us or to the people around us. But the way you reacted and dropped everything to take care of me made me feel confident that we'll be able to get through anything. You make me feel safe, and watched over, like nobody ever has before.

In fact, there is only one promise you have not kept, and it was one you made when we first met. You said I shouldn't date you, because you would break my heart. I believe my response was: "How do you know I won't break *your* heart?" And the game was on. And we both failed miserably, as evidenced by this rather public waving of the white flag.

I love how much you love your family and friends, and what a good friend you are, and what good friends you surround yourself with. I feel confident you would have realized on your own what a catch I was, but I still credit your friend Christina for punching you, fairly hard, after she met me, and telling you not to screw this up. And although you definitely have a mind of your own, I know that a veto from any one of a number of people here might have meant no party tonight. Well, you would have been at some party tonight, but not this party.

And I have to thank my friends, too, for ignoring my plea not to let me fall in love with you after you warned me I shouldn't. I remember when Liz and Elisa and Julie met you: they told me the next morning they liked us together, and they were off the case. Apparently nobody could stop this wedding from happening, not even our friends who could normally be counted on for anything.

I love what a good neighbor you are. I never had a neighbor who brought me pumpkin soufflé or green apple sorbet. I can't complain, though, because I have a boyfriend who does. A boyfriend who, even when I'm doing the lemonade fast, tells me I don't need to, then tries to make even *not eating* fun by buying a Darth Vader bendy straw, and making lemonade popsicles with ice trays and toothpicks. Of course, this generosity comes with a price. Gone forever are the days when I could, like a good New Yorker, go into my house, or walk down the street, without talking to anyone. You make friends at the shoe repair store and J&R. You know every dog that walks down our lane by name. Even those two identical dogs: you remember which one is the nice one. Which brings me to another point. You do not judge based on appearances. You are not a snob. I love that you are as impressed by a good cheese maker as you are by Sir Elton John.

Speaking of cheese, I was thinking about that first night you cooked for me, which included the first of many cheese lectures. You like to say that's how you wooed me, but that's not exactly what happened. What happened was that it was very early in our relationship. In fact, we weren't "a relationship." We were, at best, an extended booty call (and sometimes I went to your place when you were drunk instead of you showing up at mine, so we weren't even doing a booty call right), which is why I almost canceled our dinner plans that night. I was feeling tired and not in a great mood and I didn't feel like dressing up or putting on makeup and I knew we didn't have the kind of relationship where I could just come over and be myself, and I felt certain we never would, and I was thinking maybe I'd never have that, and I think I said pretty much all of that when I called to cancel. And I remember you replied, "You're a freak, but okay."

And then we hung up. And I sat there wondering if I *was* a freak, which had never really occurred to me before. So I decided to go over, no makeup, not in a great mood, and as soon as I arrived I saw you had all the ingredients you'd bought at the farmers' market on the table: the raw-milk white cheddar, the dried mushrooms reconstituting or whatever they do, and everything chopped and ready. And I'd had men cook for me before—you know, the one pasta dish they know how to make to impress a date—but this was different. You knew what you were doing, and you could do it in the tiniest of New York kitchens, and I never would have figured you for such a chef, and we had a lovely night.

And I think now about how many of those nights we've had since, and how there is nobody I would rather talk to when I am feeling less than, nobody I would rather come home to after a hard day, and how wrong I was about you and us and what we could become. And unlike most people, I love being wrong. I love thinking I know the ending and then being surprised.

I love that you pass all of the relationship tests I formulated while I was waiting to meet someone, like that you love in me what I love in myself, that you make me the best version of me, that we both think we got a great deal.

I love that you are supersmart and witty and funny and sexy, and a gifted storyteller and a crazy-good improvisational poet, and a great lawyer who cares about all the right things, including words. I love that we can agree to disagree about some issues, like the comma before the "and."

I love that once you decided we were in for the long haul, you never wavered. You never threatened to leave or used your love as leverage, as I did once or twice in a weak moment. It should be apparent to you now that I was bluffing. But you always made it clear that we were staying together, and that we had no choice but to work things out, which is an amazing quality, and one I know will serve us well throughout our lives. You basically removed the eject button.

And I love that you never let us go to bed angry. I always thought that was sort of a suggestion, but you take it very seriously, and we are better for it. I love that you hold me all night every night, and that you pull me close as soon as you wake up, and that your kiss still makes my knees weak like it did the first night we met.

I love what an adventure I know our life will continue to be. I was always worried that getting married would mean getting boring, but one thing I know is that life with you will never be boring. You always want to do more, learn more, and see more, as evidenced by the fact that last weekend, when any other couple would be putting the finishing touches on their wedding plans, we were in the pool at John Jay College getting our scuba diving certificates. And maybe it was all those years on *Sex and the City*, but I couldn't help but wonder . . . wouldn't it be nice to have a buddy system in life, and maybe that's what marriage is?

I remember worrying, when I first moved to New York, that something could happen to me and nobody would know. But now I have you, the ultimate buddy. And it makes me ridiculously, politically incorrectly happy to know you're on my team, rooting for me, watching out for me, and that you'll help me if ever there's a crisis, even though at John Jay College you swam to the surface before I got my regulator back in my mouth and my mask cleared. And even though you've been laughing all week about how I got to the surface and said (mask squashing my nose): "You're supposed to be my buddy!" Despite that lapse, I know I can count on you . . . to lose credit cards and keys but never lose sight of what's important.

I know you will be an amazing husband because you have been an amazing boyfriend and an amazing fiancé, and if all goes well, I know you will be an amazing father.

This is why you, Ian Michael Wallach, out of all the people in the world, are the man I want to spend my life with. I love you truly, madly, deeply. I love you for crying during the happy and sad scenes in movies and in life. I love you for loving me as well as you do, and for proposing in such a romantic and bold way to set the tone for this romantic and bold wedding, and a romantic and bold future.

I love you for never being halfhearted about anything, and for taking this giant step with me, and for making it easy to say out loud, in front of my closest friends and family, how much and why I love you.

Oh, How We Love Bad Boys

Agood man is not so hard to find. I've dated a bunch of them. They call when they say they're going to call, they take you out on actual dates, they tell their friends and even their parents about you, they like their parents, they play their phone messages in front of you, they have just one glass of wine with dinner because they're driving, they have jobs, they have female friends they haven't slept with . . . yeah, yeah, whatever. The point is they're not hard to find. Bad boys are hard to find, because they're never where they're supposed to be. In fact, they're not supposed to be anywhere. They do as they please. They go where the wind takes them. If you're lucky, you might get a cell phone number, so you never know exactly what (or who) a bad boy is doing. It's infuriating and insensitive and intriguing and insane and oh, how we love bad boys.

You know you're dating a bad boy when you're not sure you're actually dating. Bad boys are usually one of two things: unavailable or undressed. This leaves you unable to think of anything but where the hell is he and when will he do that to me again? Bad boys are rule breakers and heartbreakers and bed shakers and oh, how we love bad boys.

A bad boy will call you "baby," probably because he forgot your name, but still, there's nothing sexier than a bad boy who's dying to see you, baby. It doesn't matter if anything he says is true. It sounds good, and it feels good, because, baby, bad boys have throw down.

Bad boys are not tentative about kissing. They are not tentative about anything. They know what they want and they go for it, which is thrilling when it's you, and not so thrilling when it's suddenly the model (not) eating at the table next to yours. Of course, that rarely happens, because bad boys rarely take you out. They don't have to. The bar is low for bad boys. They don't have to surprise you with flowers; it's a surprise they show up at all. In fact, a bad boy is happy to let a good guy take you to dinner, ask you about you, kiss you good night at the door—a bad boy knows he can call at midnight and still get invited over for dessert.

Bad boys are dessert. They're like hot fudge sundaes. You know they're not good for you. You know that, as a woman, at a certain age, you're not supposed to indulge anymore, but that doesn't mean you won't fantasize about it while you're eating your mixed berries.

The other fantasy, of course, is that you will somehow reform a bad boy. That you will meet one with a motorcycle and tattoos and a love of bars, and he'll tell you he's trouble, but clearly that's all a front. In truth, he's just wounded, as we all are, and eventually he'll fall madly in love with you because you are what is missing in his life.

Okay, I admit it. I recently married a bad boy. The thing is, bad boys are so elusive, so aware of their options (her, her, and her), so impossible to pin down, when one gives you a ring, it means something. That you should hire a very old nanny. Oh, oh, oh, how we love bad boys.

I wrote that ode to bad boys for *People* magazine's 2005 Sexiest Man Alive issue. That year, the year Ian and I got married, the editors divided their sexy men into three categories: Smart Guys, Funny Guys, and Bad Boys, and Ian took it as the highest compliment that I included him (at least literarily) in the same category as Lenny Kravitz, Russell Crowe, and Colin Farrell.

To this day I'm still not sure if it was a compliment or a cry for help. Ian was definitely more of a bad boy than I had ever dated, but rather than run the other way, I married him.

People—not *People* magazine, but people in general—tend to think I'm overstating this bad-boy thing when they meet Ian, mostly because he seems very happily in love with me, and he now has a Vespa instead of a motorcycle. But don't let that fool you. There are ramifications when you marry a bad boy, and here is one of them: most of the women a bad boy introduces you to, he has slept with. (That's why you might make a phone call instead of small talk when he introduces you to an exotic beauty outside of Canal Jeans.) It seems like we're always in danger of running into someone Ian slept with, usually when I'm looking my worst. After a long international flight, on the shuttle bus to the parking lot, Ian will say, "Oh my God, Cookie?!" (yes, her real name), and then from what they say—or don't say—about how they know each other, I can tell she's someone he slept with before we met.

Incidentally, we are still friends with Cookie and many other Cookies from Ian's past. But for some reason, I like to know—I *need* to know—if these women had sex with my husband.

It would probably be healthier not to know, not to keep this tally in my head. He married me, after all. But knowing makes me feel like these ghosts of his sexual past do not have the upper hand. He does not share a secret with them. He shares their secret with me.

I leave it to you to figure out if that makes me highly evolved or highly masochistic, but I will say that this is a hell of my own making, because Ian is not, by nature, a kiss-and-teller. He never points out that a woman is someone he slept with (maybe because, at some point, I should just assume), but if I ask him about it later, he always answers honestly, usually positively and dismissively:

"Once, when I was in high school."

"We were working together."

"The bride doesn't count." (I'd asked if there would be anyone he'd slept with at a wedding we were attending.)

"I was living in Paris."

"She was angry with her husband."

Or my personal favorite: "I never slept with Twinkie [not her real name]. But I once held my ex while Twinkie went down on her, because my ex always had kind of a lesbian fantasy of that."

That last one caught me off guard (as I'm sure it just did my parents, Twinkie, and Ian's ex, if they are reading this), and it was probably an indication that I should stop asking questions I might not want to know the answer to. That rule is a good one in court and in marriage. In fact, I'm still recovering from that particular answer. I am sorry for asking, sorry for knowing, sorry you have to know, and sorry that I will never be as sexually adventurous as Ian's ex. Yes, I understand, never say never, but I am pretty sure no matter where life takes us, I will not be asking Ian to hold me while some other Twinkie goes down on me. And if that did happen, which it wouldn't, but let's just say it did, we would not still be friends with my Twinkie and exchange holiday cards and know her husband and kids. But this is how it is for bad boys. It's all in the past. He married *me*.

I think the dream of monogamy pretty much died for most women when Hugh Grant cheated on Elizabeth Hurley.

I mean, if a man can't stay faithful to Elizabeth Hurley, what hope do the rest of us have? Ian tells me he doesn't find Elizabeth Hurley so attractive. I don't find that comforting. All that says to me is that if Elizabeth Hurley is not so attractive, the rest of us are even less attractive than I thought.

In any case, Ian's sexual past is not a huge part of my everyday consciousness. But my subconscious, especially right after we got married, was having a field day with it.

My subconscious was especially concerned with what Ian had told me when we first met—that he might never get married (red flag) because he wasn't sure he believed in monogamy (bigger red flag), but if he did get married, maybe it would be to a Russian mail-order bride (there is not a flag big enough or red enough for that comment).

But then Ian surpassed all of my expectations and turned out to be a great guy.

Except at night. In my dreams. There Ian was everything you would fear a bad-boy husband would be. He would kiss women right in front of me; he would announce he was leaving me; sometimes he would just ignore me. He would have twosomes, threesomes, foursomes as if I wasn't there, even though I *was* there (it being my dream and all), standing by, reminding Ian that I was his wife, that we were married, that this was inappropriate behavior for a husband.

I would wake up hurt and upset and confront Ian with everything he had done. And that's when we started calling this man of my dreams "Evil Ian," because the real Ian pointed out that he had, in fact, done nothing wrong, given me no reason to have these nightmares, been a great husband from day one. But Evil Ian continued to haunt and taunt me.

Ian started to resent his evil counterpart. "He has all the fun, and I get all the blame," Ian complained one morning as

I recounted what Evil Ian had done with some hottie on a cruise ship.

And it was true. Where was Ian's reward for going from motorcycle to Vespa if I still woke up angry? Was my subconscious trying to protect me or sabotage me?

If you are a therapist reading this, or even if you aren't, I'm sure it's not hard to figure out that I was having trust issues. I'd been disappointed by men in the past, so when Ian told me up front that he was bad news, I took him at his word.

But here's the thing: Ian was *not* the guy he said he was. He was better than he said he was. Which was enough to blow your mind if you'd been dating as long as I had. Nobody is better than he says he is. One online date will confirm that for you.

So my subconscious was, I guess, trying to work out how a bad boy could be so good. Ian *was* a good man, a good husband, a good lover, and even a good sport as I continued to love and trust him by day and curse Evil Ian by night.

Eventually, my Evil Ian dreams began to subside, which was a relief, because not only was it unfair to Ian, it was unfair to me. If anyone was going to have extramarital sex in my dreams, it should be me. And monogamy is no small undertaking. Men are not the only ones who have trouble adjusting to the idea of sex with the same person day after day, night after night (well, at first; then it's more like month after month), and yet, I wasn't even cheating in my dreams. Where was the honor in that?

All I can imagine is that I have been faithful, consciously and subconsciously, because the man of my dreams is now the same man I wake up to. The real Ian finally eclipsed Evil Ian.

Of course, he's still a bad boy at heart. And in some twisted, unhealthy way, that's why he's so dreamy.

In Sickness and in Health

It was recently pointed out to me that when it comes to dealing with illness in our marriage, Ian is the more nurturing
one. The fact that it was Ian who pointed this out (and it
wasn't the first time he's done so) makes me feel he should
lose a few nurturing points. I can't imagine Mother Teresa
bragging about how much more nurturing she was than everyone else in the leper colony, but, putting that aside, I have
noticed that whenever I wake up with a sore throat or cold,
Ian rises to the occasion almost eagerly, heating water for
Theraflu, arming me with the remote, plying me with vitamin
C, and getting chicken soup or sometimes even *making*
chicken soup.

I am reluctant to mention this other thing—my "dingaling
privileges"—because Ian sounds disproportionately devoted
(or deranged) already. But there have been times while we were
trying to get pregnant that I was bedridden (sometimes for
hopeful reasons, sometimes for tragic ones), and in order to

keep my spirits up, Ian announced that anytime I called, "Dingaling!" he would rush to my bedside, respond, "Yes, my love?" and do whatever I asked. Then one year he took it a step further and got me an actual brass dinner bell engraved with the words "Cindy's Dingaling Privileges," which he said I could ring whenever I was sick, or for the full nine months if I did get pregnant.

Wow, right? I know. It's not as sugary sweet as it sounds (well, maybe it is), but I would at least like to assure you that the bell has not been abused by me, or used for sexual favors (which would make for better reading), and I would now like to unring that bell and have you forget I ever mentioned it except as an example of how over-the-top kind Ian can be when he is called upon to nurture.

I, on the other hand, and somewhat to my surprise, do not enjoy taking care of a sick husband as much as I had imagined I might. I had visions of bringing my spouse soup on a tray accompanied by a flower in a bud vase and a carefully folded newspaper, like movie spouses do. Like Ian does. But that was not to be.

I would like to believe I will get better at nurturing with age (it will certainly become more necessary with age), but despite the example Ian set with the kindness of the bell (damn that bell!), I maintain that there is something about seeing your husband with a cold (even if he's a very nice husband) that is just not appealing.

Of course, if Ian were seriously ill, that would be another matter. If he had something life-threatening or immobilizing,

I feel certain I would rise to the occasion as I have for many friends over the years, but we're talking about a cold.

I would like to add here that I rarely get sick. I get sick maybe once every year or two, and only for a few days. So taking care of me could be considered almost a novelty.

Ian seems to get sick more often ("like a regular person," he would insist, because he thinks it's weird that I get sick so infrequently). But when the fuzzy sock is on the other foot, when I wake to hear him sneezing in sets of seven without covering his mouth, coughing seemingly for dramatic effect, unable to open his eyes when he hoarsely talks—especially if he was out drinking the night before (which is sometimes the case, in my defense)—he just seems . . . weak.

And he *is* weak at that moment, I know! He is legitimately weak and compromised and in need of love and nurturing, and for some reason I find this state so unattractive in a spouse, especially a male spouse, that it renders me unable to be as kind and empathetic as I should be.

By now it should be clear that I don't deserve a husband, let alone a bell. If it helps, I am as shocked and disappointed by this failure as Ian probably was. Until I got married, I was completely unaware that I had this bitchy inner nurse who just wants everyone to get up and get back to business, but I do, and—what can I say?—she hates her job.

Meanwhile, who would have thought that Ian, the guy who said he didn't even want a relationship, would turn out to be such a loving, caring knight in shining armor, literally?

Luckily, or unluckily, I didn't have to wait until I married him to find that out. I discovered it right before our wedding, on my fortieth birthday, because on my fortieth birthday I got a mammogram.

Not as a gift. And not as a celebration, in the way that you might get a tattoo on your birthday, or go skydiving. It wasn't something I had always wanted to do. I simply had made a routine appointment at Sloan-Kettering in New York, and I didn't appreciate the lameness of the timing until the receptionist asked for my date of birth.

As she wished me a happy birthday, I was reminded of a time, decades earlier, when I first moved to Los Angeles. I was taking a stand-up comedy workshop, and although my 99 Cents store bit was a crowd-pleaser (the "crowd" in this case being the four to five people who were not taking a turn at the mic), it soon became clear that I was a better writer than performer, so a girl in the class asked me to write jokes for her. And that girl was . . . nobody you've heard of, because she wasn't that good, and neither were my jokes. But by way of thanking me, she took me to this trendy restaurant, and for some reason she showed up looking as if she hadn't showered for days, with no makeup and hair under a scarf. She was slightly strange to begin with, but she usually showered, so this seemed odd. Especially since we were at a trendy restaurant of her choosing.

Now maybe, since I mentioned mammograms, you're thinking this is going to be about how she was getting chemo and losing her hair, thus the scarf. It's not that poignant of a story.

It's about my birthday, because she decided to lie and tell our waiter it was my birthday so he would bring us a free dessert, and as he and the rest of the waitstaff were singing, I was thinking what a sad fake birthday this was. Why would I be out with only my one weird friend (who didn't even shower) on my birthday? Where were the rest of my fake friends? And my fake boyfriend? And the fake gifts? Even back then, with no fabulousness to back me up, I felt too fabulous for that fake birthday.

So now, at forty, I was definitely too fabulous to be getting a mammogram on my actual birthday. But there I was at Sloan-Kettering, putting on the cotton robe and waiting for my name to be called.

I have some close friends who are breast cancer survivors, and they all benefited greatly from early detection, so I am a believer in the power of the breast sandwich.

That's what it looks like when you get a mammogram, by the way. Especially if you have large breasts, which I do. I don't say that to brag. I would be perfectly happy, maybe happier, with perky breasts, but I was blessed (or cursed) with large ones. Of course, I did not know how large they were until, at age thirty-seven, I got my first mammogram, and they were spread out before me in all their flat, fleshy glory. Once, when I was seventeen, I went skydiving, and I can tell you that looking down at the ground from 3,500 feet was not as scary as looking down at my breast sandwich. So, my advice to women who want to live longer and be healthier and happier: do not avoid mammograms, but do avoid looking down when getting one.

Since that first mammogram (which, thankfully, came back normal), my health insurance had changed its policy so that you had to be forty to get a mammogram covered—even though you don't have to be forty to get breast cancer, thank you very much. In fact, that's what I argued to some poor, overworked insurance claims person when I called to see why I had to wait. She explained that insurance requirements vary state to state, carrier to carrier, blah blah blah. So anyhow, that's how I came to be at Sloan-Kettering on my fortieth birthday.

Well, that and also, as I mentioned, I was getting married in a month, and my life was so full of appointments and plans that I hadn't really thought about what I was scheduling, or when. I only thought about how I could check something, anything, off my to-do list, and eliminating the possibility of breast cancer was a good candidate.

Only that's not what happened.

The appointment itself went fine, especially since I knew not to look down this time around. And the rest of my birthday was lovely. (Where is there to go but up after a mammogram, really?) But the next day I got a call from Sloan-Kettering saying something was irregular with my left breast, and I needed to come back as soon as possible. "Irregular" and "as soon as possible" are not words you want to hear from a doctor's office. Even just "left breast"—you don't want a breast singled out. Breasts come in pairs, and when all is going well, they are treated as pairs.

I immediately began seeing my life as a bad TV movie. I

would be a bald bride walking down the aisle, and everyone would be saying how brave I was instead of how beautiful and happy. I imagined the wedding planning getting sidetracked by doctor's appointments, maybe even the wedding itself getting sidetracked, maybe the wedding being moved up so I could get married before I left the planet. By the time I called Ian at work (thirty seconds later) I was in tears and practically writing my obit.

This was not the first time I'd assumed the worst when it came to my health. At fifteen in the town where I grew up—Tulsa, Oklahoma—I'd secretly plotted for a week how to get to Planned Parenthood to see if I had a sexually transmitted disease. I finally rode my bike there (not a short ride) to learn that not only did I not have the disease, I did not have *sex*. Or "penetration," as the nurse delicately called it as she rattled through her standard questions. When I asked what that meant exactly, it became clear to her (and me) that the naked fumbling I'd done recently did not count, and to add insult to virginity, she said the blister I was concerned about was most likely from my thighs rubbing together when I walked. So I had cellulite, not syphilis.

Despite that early lesson on not jumping to conclusions, I leapt. In my mind, if not in my breast, I had cancer. Or at least the possibility of cancer. And in that uncertainty, I understood what it meant to be terrified. To know that one test, one call from a doctor, could change your life forever. Thankfully, Ian calmed me down. He said, "Not on my watch. Nothing is going to happen to you on my watch." That was so sweet and comforting, but it did not stop me from wondering, as he held me in his arms that night, *Who the hell does he think he is? A superhero?! You can't stop cancer from happening, no matter how much you love someone!*

In my fear I felt as if I was totally and irreversibly on my own. Those words had been echoing in my ears ever since my skydiving instructor had said, "When you leave this plane, you are totally and irreversibly on your own." It wasn't a tandem jump I had done, but a static cord, so I was, in fact, on my own. And as I floated past the soft green grass of a landing field where you were supposed to land, and headed toward the parking lot of cars, where you were not supposed to land, I realized "on your own" was not the best place for me to be.

While I was attempting to steer (there were cords you could pull to turn slightly right or left), I looked for the giant arrow on the ground that the people who worked there had turned to point me in the right direction for landing, and the parking lot was in the direction the giant arrow was pointing. What I failed to notice (since I was totally and irreversibly on my own) was that, at a certain point, they had turned the arrow in the opposite direction so that I would be heading into the wind, which naturally slows you down. By the time I finally did notice it, it was too late, and I was too low. I remember people yelling supportive things like, "Don't land on my car!" and I remember that instead of the five-point landing we had practiced over and over (feet, calf muscle, thigh muscle, buttocks, push-up muscle), I did a one-point landing, on my butt, directly onto the gravel.

So I was not so good on my own. And cancer seemed like something you had to do completely on your own, because in the end, it's a battle inside your own body.

Ian went with me to the follow-up appointment, and this time when I got the mammogram, it was all about the left breast. There were more angles, and more care was taken to get the X-rays exactly right. Then we were told to wait in a special room for results, which looked like a living room, because . . . hopefully I would be?

There was another couple in the room. They were older. They seemed as if they'd been through this before, as if this testing and waiting were part of their lives now, and I feared we might be destined to become people for whom this would become routine as well.

After what seemed like an eternity (twenty minutes?), the nurse asked me to follow her back into the exam area. I remember that Ian did not want to let go of my hand. I thought they might need more film taken, but instead, a female radiologist was waiting to see me. She was sitting in front of my X-rays, which were black and blue and lit from behind. My heart dropped. But she immediately alleviated my worries and told me I was fine. She showed me what had troubled her in the first X-ray, and how the new ones had confirmed that it was just something on the film, or the angle at which the photo was taken. To be honest, I'm not sure what she said. I don't think I heard anything after "You're fine."

So what I learned at forty, a few weeks before my wedding, was that Ian would indeed be a good partner in sickness and in health. He dropped everything to be by my side, and when I emerged from the exam area to tell him I was okay, he cried. It was the first and only sign that he had been as worried as I had been. If he'd had tears and fears before that, he'd kept them to himself.

I also got a tiny taste of what so many of my friends with cancer have gone through and continue to go through every time they see a doctor, not to mention all of the anxious hours and years in between. I feel kind of ridiculous telling this story in light of the real drama my friends and their partners and families have bravely faced. But I think it made me a better person, to appreciate how precious health is, and how everything could change in an instant, and how, even though the people who love you can't stop difficult things from happening, they will be there when you need them, every scary step of the way.

And I will be there for Ian if he ever faces something scary. I know that I will.

But colds are not scary.

People do not tell you that they are a cold survivor.

You are not a hero for bravely fighting a cold, and you are not a saint for helping your loved one fight a cold.

There will never be a television show called *The Big C* about a woman living with a cold.

Maybe that's why it's all the more impressive that Ian is

there for me during the colds as well. Maybe I need to try harder. Maybe I will give him dingaling privileges the next time he is sick. Maybe I'll make him soup, and bring it to him on a tray with a flower and newspaper.

But I doubt it.

Self-Storage

One dilemma I remember wrestling with as a single woman was whether or not to buy a house. I know that's a luxury problem (like faux fur or no fur), but it was still a very fraught decision, made more fraught by all of the unsolicited and conflicting opinions I got on the topic. And those were just the ones in my head.

Half of me was certain I was better off as a modular unit that could be picked up and moved easily into someone else's life, and in that scenario, real estate would only complicate my whirlwind romance.

The other half of me asked, *What whirlwind romance?*

The truth is, there was nobody in the picture when I was thinking of looking at houses, and there hadn't been anyone for some time who hadn't had either a fear of commitment or a prior commitment (an old girlfriend, a wife), so the only whirlwind I was experiencing was that, while I was debating the pros and cons of home ownership as a single woman, married women were snatching up all the hot properties.

Yes, the Real Housewives of Beverly Hills–adjacent were at every open house the minute it opened, calling their husbands, describing the place room by room while I was still racing to get to the listing before my lunch hour ended. I resented these ladies at first, these hoarders of the good men and the good houses, until I realized that I was in an enviable position. I didn't need a handsome man in an expensive suit with an adorable son on his shoulders to saunter in and kiss me and sign the paperwork.

I wanted one, but I didn't *need* one. At least, not to buy a house.

So I did it. On my own. Because I could. And maybe partially because my mom had never had that chance. My mom lived with her mother until she was married. She never got to turn a sunroom into an art studio, or design her dream kitchen. She's still rarely allowed to buy a piece of furniture on a whim. She defers to my dad on these matters, not because he has the taste, but because he makes the money. If my dad wanted a green leather couch, they got a green leather couch. Sadly, that's not my way of explaining that he got what he wanted; that's my way of telling you that my parents have a green leather couch.

But, thankfully, I do not. I found a gorgeous, modern condo at the beach, and by some miracle it was the perfect time to buy, and it's beautifully decorated to my specifications, and it was a great bachelorette pad, and I had amazing parties there, and when people complimented my home (which was deemed "the Fabulous Beach House"), I would say brightly: "All that's missing is the guy."

What I didn't realize was that the guy, when he finally did come, would come with *things*.

And the Fabulous Beach House wasn't lacking *things*. Especially things like a remote-control helicopter and a samurai sword and a large wooden chess set that Ian's brother had made, let alone art that I didn't particularly like, and stereo equipment that needed fixing, and a pinball machine that was all Ian had left of a father who had died when Ian was ten.

Okay, the pinball machine we'd find space for, but certainly not everything qualified as sentimental. For example, the remote-control helicopter, I knew for a fact, was brand new. Ian got it to celebrate the high ceilings in my house, which was now "our house," which is why Ian needed space for his clothes and pinball machine and whatever the hell else was coming in box after box after box.

This is how I found myself looking at storage units. I know that Suze Orman and pretty much every other smart person on the planet agrees that storage units are a huge waste of money. Why pay rent for things you aren't using, things you will one day forget you have?

Here's why: there is a man in my house—our house—and I married him.

This is probably why couples should buy a house together, although maybe men who own their own homes enjoy having a woman move in. It probably makes a man feel as if he is providing for his spouse. I thought about why it was different for me. Was it sexist? Did I secretly wish Ian had brought a house to the table?

No. I wished Ian had brought *nothing* to the table, including the table.

I loved Ian. I just didn't love his things.

Now, before you deem me a snob, I would like to explain that I did live with Ian in his very small Lower East Side apartment for a few months while we were dating.

I'd been working in New York and living in a furnished apartment, but my lease was up, and my job was ending, and it seemed encouraging and astounding that my bad-boy boyfriend wanted me to stay and live with him. So I decided to ignore his scary bathroom and tiny bedroom and complete lack of closet space. We could do this. We were in love.

Ian built shelves above the bed for my shoes. He cooked me delicious meals in the hallway he called a kitchen. We went to the farmers' market together every Sunday. We were the New York couple I always wanted to be. And at night as his radiator rattled and clanged, I would lie in his arms and look up at my shoes and think/sing: *We gotta get out of this place.*

According to Wikipedia, "We Gotta Get Out of This Place" by the Animals was immensely popular among United States armed forces during the Vietnam War. I'm not likening my situation on the Lower East Side to Vietnam, but I will say the lack of an exit strategy was starting to worry me.

The final straw was the NYU students. Ian's lease was almost up, and the apartment was being shown, and while I was home making the bed by standing on top of it (which is how you had to do it, since it took up half of the room), two young Asian students came in, took a quick look around, and announced, "This isn't big enough for two people." They were eighteen-year-old girls. And not to stereotype, but Asian girls are by and large not large people.

I decided—much as I had about the backpacking I was willing to do early in our relationship because I was so excited Ian wanted to travel with me—that I was too old for this crap.

I had tried. I had showered in a shower that seemed impervious to cleaning products. Its best bet was that it might end up in the public garden next door with the other discarded bathroom fixtures that were trying to pass as art. We had to get out of that place.

And we did. We rented a West Village apartment together for a year, and then Ian proposed, and now he was leaving everything behind (well, he was leaving New York behind—the rest he had apparently brought with him) to join me in Los Angeles, because I had a career and house there.

And that house was perfect as is! That's what I was thinking as I took the large metal elevator to my potential storage unit. That house was once featured in *InStyle Home*, and, aside from some slight restaging—apparently I needed aqua ceramic vases, an orange cashmere blanket, and a breakfast tray with books on it—it was clearly considered a lovely space by people who specialized in lovely spaces, so why mess with it?

Because I was now married. That's why.

That's what I kept coming back to.

Ian wasn't just visiting. He wasn't a booty call (anymore). He was my husband, and I needed to make room for him, emotionally and physically.

So I put some of my things in storage, including my beloved art deco bedroom and vanity set with Bakelite handles that I had bought when my first marriage was ending. I remember my soon-to-be-ex-husband saying "You don't have room for that furniture," while I was thinking *I will when you leave*. Now that art deco declaration of independence was leaning against a wall in unit R3176, along with my grandmother's bentwood rocking chair and a bunch of expensive throw pillows.

I had no idea I had so many throw pillows. Why doesn't Suze Orman warn people about those? They cost a small fortune, they have to be literally thrown aside so you can enjoy the furniture they adorn, and eventually they adorn your storage unit.

As I was about to lock the unit up, I thought: *It's not bad in here. If you set it up right, you could sit quietly among your things. You could use it as an office. It could be like a home away from home. Maybe this is where I will go when I need space.*

Then it hit me: why was I looking for a space to be alone in, when I had waited so long to find someone to share my space with so I *wouldn't* be alone?

And then everything went black.

The lights, it turned out, were on a timer in these storage units. That would definitely be a problem as far as using mine for an office. Apparently I would have to find space for Ian, Ian's things, and me in our house. And in the years to come, I thought, if we're lucky enough to expand our family, we'll pack up our things and, together, we will look for a bigger storage unit.

The First No No Noel

Iblame the Pottery Barn holiday catalog for the fact that Ian and I, both Jews, kicked off one of our first holiday seasons as a married couple at Home Depot, picking out a Christmas tree. I cannot blame our kids, who begged us mercilessly for a Christmas tree, because we did not yet have kids. I cannot blame my parents, because although my dad initially supported Bush (one and two), he never supported the Hanukkah bush. In fact, I recall that he was extremely judgmental of one Jewish family in our predominantly non-Jewish hometown of Tulsa who did have a Christmas tree every year. Even though it was decorated exclusively with blue ornaments and silver bows, my dad made it clear to my sister and me that he thought the whole "Jews with Trees" movement was in very poor taste.

Then again, my dad was a man who, in his wood-paneled wet bar, had highball glasses featuring busty women whose clothes disappeared when the glass was full. So I learned early on that taste was subjective.

Fast-forward to November 2006. Ian and I had been married a year and a half, and I was flipping through the Pottery Barn holiday catalog, with page after page featuring something beautiful but not for us, because we were Jews. In my opinion, Jews have yet to make Hanukkah decor beautiful, unless you consider a blue and white paper dreidel beautiful, but what can you expect from a holiday whose spelling is annually up for debate?

So as I browsed past monogrammed velvet stockings and quilted tree skirts and pinecone wreaths and silver-plated picture frames that doubled as stocking holders (genius!), I said to Ian, "This is why I sometimes wish I celebrated Christmas. Everything looks so cozy and inviting." And much to my surprise, he replied, "We can celebrate Christmas, if you want." And, like a twelve-year-old, I said, "We can?" And he said, "Sure."

It seemed so subversive. Christmas? *Really?* I thought about it for a moment. Or rather, I thought about what my parents would think. But my parents were 1,200 miles away. They weren't visiting that season. They wouldn't even need to know. (Until now. Merry Christmas, Mom and Dad!) Still, even just considering the possibility felt wrong and dirty and . . . totally exhilarating, like your first night away at college, when you realize you can stay out until dawn because nobody is waiting up for you. Ian and I were consenting adults. We were married. This was our home. Why couldn't we celebrate whatever the hell we wanted?

We decided we could, and proceeded to embrace the

holiday in all of its commercial glory. For example, while I know it can be annoying to Christmas veterans, I discovered there is nothing I love more than hearing "Rudolph the Red-Nosed Reindeer" while shopping for stocking stuffers. I love stocking stuffers. I love having stockings to stuff. I love that whole sections of stores, from CVS to Neiman Marcus, suddenly opened up to me. I love tinsel. It's so simple, yet so elegant! I love that as soon as I told a Catholic friend what I was up to, she invited me to a gingerbread-house decorating party. How fun is *that*? And why hadn't I been invited before? What does a gingerbread house have to do with Jesus?

So there we were: two newlywed Jews celebrating our No No Noel (or Ho Ho Hanukkah) with no excuse other than the fact that I wanted monogrammed velvet stockings and Ian wanted—it turned out—the train set that goes around the tree and puffs actual smoke.

That train (which took two hours to assemble) was the first sign that our Christmas might not be all peace on earth, goodwill toward men. The vision dancing in my head was clearly Pottery Barn, whereas Ian's, I fear, was SkyMall.

He bought colored blinking lights when I was definitely thinking white, and he ordered old-timey glass ornaments—a slice of pizza, a mermaid, a hippo—instead of the understated jewel-colored balls that I had in mind. Plus he kept talking about the fake snow ("Should we get the blanket or just use cotton balls?") when I wasn't thinking fake snow at all. I definitely hadn't seen any fake snow in the Pottery Barn catalog. And then at Home Depot, I practically had to pry the mechanical lawn snowman out of his hands. Ian was like a Christmas crackhead . . . one taste, and he couldn't stop.

But despite our differences, we both loved the little winter wonderland we finally settled on. Some nights when I got home before Ian, I put on our Starbucks Christmas CD and lit a fire and turned on the tree lights and played with the different settings (disco fast, then twinkly slow) and put liquid smoke in the train's smokestack and turned on the choo-choo sound effects and then sat back and enjoyed my first Christmas in all its kitschy splendor. I felt a little guilty when I looked at our lone menorah on the mantel (the only evidence of my faith other than my guilt), but I ask you: how could this much pleasure be wrong?

Before you answer that, fellow Jews (including you, Dad), let me just say that Ian and I were fairly certain that once we had kids, we would raise them with the same rules we were raised with, trying our best to sell that old chestnut (roasting on an open fire) that "eight nights are better than one," and putting this tradition behind us until the kids went off to college, if not forever. It seemed easy enough to hide the evidence. I accidentally dropped an old-timey basket-of-cherries ornament, and it shattered into a powder so fine there was no trace it ever existed.

On the other hand, I started to wonder if it might be nice to teach children that holidays can be done à la carte. Every religion, every culture, has so many beautiful rituals and traditions. Maybe celebrating is a step toward tolerating. Maybe our family would ring in Hanukkwanzaa.

Or maybe I was rationalizing because I had become so intoxicated by the scent of pine needles and poinsettias that I couldn't imagine life without them! Just as once you fly first class, it's hard to go back to coach—once you have Christmas, it's hard to go back to no Christmas.

That's why we have the ornaments, the lights, the train, the stockings, and the giant inflatable lawn penguin (Ian's idea, in case there was any question) in storage unit R3176. No No Noel has become a tradition for us, not instead of Hanukkah, but in addition. It's no longer a novelty, but . . . we like it, okay?

And marriage, for better or worse, means you have a full-time, live-in enabler. That's one of my favorite aspects of marriage, actually—the fact that your partner in life can be your partner in crime. Together, you can create new traditions, make your own rules, and break your own rules.

Christmas isn't the only holiday Ian and I bent to our will. We started out, as most couples do, trying to alternate Thanksgivings between our families. One year we'd go to Dallas (where my sister and parents now live), the next we'd go to Pittsburgh (where Ian's brother was doing his medical residency), and so on and so on—our plan until we had kids of our own, at which point people might finally come to us so we could *not* travel on the busiest travel day of the year.

But one year, still kidless, we were both on a strict diet,

and we were trying to figure out how we would stay on that diet during Thanksgiving, and we finally broke with tradition like two crazy rebels and announced that we were staying in Los Angeles and cooking our own low-cal but delicious Thanksgiving dinner, for just the two of us.

Our families were disappointed, but they understood, because we were making a life together. People seem to respect that, especially people who have been waiting a long time for you to make a life with someone (and waiting even longer for you and that someone to make another life: a grandchild).

Ian cooked a pheasant instead of a turkey, and we made healthy side dishes that were steamed instead of mashed and marshmallowed, and I put mini-gourds in a bowl and tea lights on the table, and we enjoyed this small bird for two, this small feast for two, this small step toward creating independence as a couple.

And the next morning, when we opened the fridge, there were no leftovers to tempt us—no cold turkey, stuffing, yams, and cranberry sauce with which to make a 12,000-calorie sandwich . . . no leftover pumpkin pie to eat directly out of the tin until it was reduced to crumbs.

It was *bleak*.

What were we thinking? Thanksgiving happens once a year, and we had traded our corn bread for Wasa crackers? I wanted to cry. Ian wanted to eat.

We immediately fled to a nearby diner—this being Los Angeles, it was a restaurant in a strip mall made to look like a diner—and each had a turkey sandwich (dry) and slice of pumpkin pie (subpar) and vowed never to miss Thanksgiving again.

In fact, the following year we went to my sister's house and enjoyed the highest-calorie, most delicious Thanksgiving meal ever. And Ian and I cooked, not only for ourselves, but for everyone, which was a surprise to my family because they didn't know I could cook.

Frankly, *I* didn't know I could cook until I met Ian (see next chapter), but for that transformation I blame the Williams-Sonoma catalog. Those individual soufflé ramekins, the pink mixer/pasta-maker combo, the meat slicer Ian insisted we have on our registry. Yes, we now own a meat slicer, so when I buy something like prosciutto at the deli, I have to say, "I don't need it sliced, thank you; we have a meat slicer at home." I might as well be saying "Just give me the whole cow please, the whole *live* cow; we want to make our own milk."

I never thought I'd have a meat slicer.

I never thought I'd cook.

I never thought I'd be asked by a young midwestern birth mother, years later, if we'd be willing to celebrate Christmas, but since we had the decorations already . . .

I never thought I'd be asked if we'd be willing to celebrate Easter, too, but after five years of our own egg hunt trying to find one that would produce a child, Ian and I were almost willing to accept Jesus as our savior in order to complete our family. What's a little chocolate, I thought? A few Peeps? Does Easter have to be about Jesus? I don't remember seeing Jesus in the Williams-Sonoma *or* Pottery Barn Easter catalog.

But I'm getting ahead of myself. It was still early in our relationship, and we were just getting cooking. . . .

Now We're Cooking?

Name your favorite four ingredients, and we'll build a meal around them." Ian proposed this challenge to our friend Kimberly early in our marriage.

I was dubious. Ian was good in the kitchen, but he was no Iron Chef, and I grew up thinking basic ingredients were Lipton onion soup mix, Fritos, French dressing, and Bisquick. I still have recipes from my sister that call for Dr. Pepper or root beer in things like briskets and cakes, but thanks to the great restaurants of New York, Los Angeles, and beyond (famous and hole-in-the-wall ethnic), I now know that green beans can exist outside of a casserole, that most people don't even call them green beans, and that the best recipes don't have "surprise" in their names.

Before I married Ian, the only dish I felt completely confident making was chocolate chip cookies. I'm not apologizing—I make *great* cookies, sweet and salty and perfectly undercooked and chewy, but I never strayed from our family recipe. I did, one day, realize that our family recipe was eerily similar to the one printed on the package of Nestlé Toll House Semi-Sweet Chocolate Morsels, which were an *ingredient* in our family recipe, so nobody even thought to hide the evidence. Apparently it wasn't necessary, because it's only right at this moment, as I'm writing this, that I'm remembering it was not a family "chocolate chip cookie" recipe; it was a family "Toll House cookie" recipe, which, I guess, should have tipped me off, but I always thought Toll House cookies were chocolate chip cookies and vice versa, in the same way that Kleenex are tissues to everyone except people working at rival tissue companies. And still, even after discovering that the Chupack cookie legacy was, literally, ripped off a bag of chocolate chips (with one important modification: we were using Crisco instead of butter, thus making the cookies even more fattening than usual), I never so much as substituted butterscotch chips for chocolate—that's what a culinary coward I was when I was single.

My cowardice didn't stop me from throwing dinner parties, especially while I was living in New York, but at my parties the entire spread (except for our fraudulent family cookies) was from Balducci's. At one such dinner party, a friend who is an excellent cook walked in on me heating up slices of store-bought London broil. As I pulled the baking sheet out of the oven, revealing the grayish-brown meat, he looked at me as if I had just wrecked a Porsche. I think there were tears in his eyes. London broil, I now understand, should be served gorgeously medium rare, and the difference between "heating something up" and "cooking it" is not an insignificant one.

But since that first delicious evening with Kimberly (she chose as her four ingredients: pear, brie, chocolate, and her grandmother's apple pie), the "four-ingredient meal" has become Ian's favorite mode of entertaining and my favorite extreme sport. Here's how it works:

Step One: Invite. You need to be comfortable bragging, as Ian is. I can now count on him to offer up a four-ingredient meal to any of our friends, friends of friends, colleagues, and even famous people we barely know who happen to mention a fondness for food. His offer, and their subsequent acceptance (which is inevitable, because he makes the prospect sound so delectable), always sends me into a panic, even though every four-ingredient meal we've done to date has been much tastier than I ever could have imagined.

Step Two: Panic. It would be lovely not to panic, but I fear "fear" is part of my process. Panic leads to creativity. This is true in everything I do, from writing to cooking. For me, lack of panic means lack of caring. Thanks to panic, I find myself up late at night (while Ian peacefully sleeps) Googling various combinations of our guests' requested ingredients, like "rhubarb and balsamic vinegar" or "pomegranate and duck" to find inspiration and direction. I read indexes of never-cracked-open cookbooks to see which dishes call for figs or pistachio nuts. I visit stores that sell only spices, sections of the supermarket that I never knew existed, or my new favorite gourmet shop, where I will find myself debating the merits of various forms of ingredients, like truffle paste, truffle carpaccio, truffle salt, and truffle oil. I will ask the produce people which pears are best this time of year, and they will have helpful and well-reasoned answers. I will go to the farmers' market (a real one, not the one that is now part of an outdoor mall on Fairfax), where I'll discuss heirloom tomatoes with the folks who grew them. I will buy fresh parsley, sage, rosemary, and thyme (while humming the song, of course), amazed that I ever used the dry versions. Somehow this new language—food—allows me to engage in long, passionate, mouthwatering conversations with anybody, anywhere, anytime.

That is something else I never cared to do before I married Ian. I would like to say that Ian taught me the beauty of talking to strangers, but the truth is, marrying someone means that even if you didn't used to want to talk to strangers, you may want to start talking to strangers, because, unlike your husband, they at least have something new to say.

Is that terrible? Am I a terrible person? I love Ian's stories. But I have heard most of them. And he has heard most of mine. Let's listen to a stranger for a while. Let's invite friends over. Let's have a dinner party! Let's make new stories!

Step Three: Apologize. To Ian. For what I just said, since he has heard *my* stories over and over, even read them over and over, and he's still allowing me to share my stories about him in this book.

But since I brought it up (she says, unable to let it go), I do find this to be a very confusing part of partnership, which inevitably comes up when you're entertaining together. I'm a good storyteller, Ian's a good storyteller, we met at a storytelling event, so who knew my biggest question about marriage would be: what the hell am I supposed to do when Ian is telling friends a story I've heard a million times? Am I supposed to pretend I've never heard it? Should I say, "Oh, this is a great one!" (whether it is or not) so I don't have to hang on to every word like everybody else? Can I go to the bathroom or clear dishes instead? Can I start my own conversation, or is that rude, because I'm depriving someone else of his story? What if I know that other people at the table already know the story? Am I allowed to say that? Can I finish it for him? Where is the book that answers these questions? Is it supposed to be *this* book? I hope not, because I don't know the answer, just like I don't know how I ended up preparing dishes my family has never heard of for people they *have* heard of, like the Chilled Cauliflower Soup with Sevruga Caviar that I whipped up—in eight hours—for Lisa Kudrow and her husband. (We met them at a friend's wedding in Colorado, and by the reception, Ian had invited them to dinner.)

Incidentally, Lisa Kudrow and her husband seemed genuinely delighted and entertained by each other's stories, as were we (by their stories), although I didn't get to participate in the talking as much I would have liked, because I got completely carried away with (and intimidated by) my own menu planning.

Step Four: Plan. Like I said, we are not Iron Chefs. We need more than an hour to plan (not to mention shop for) a meal, especially if *someone* (Ian) decides the duck needs to be bought in Chinatown. Or if that same someone further complicates the challenge by promising to use the ingredients "in an unexpected way."

For example, at our first four-ingredient meal, Kimberly's grandmother's apple pie became an apple martini with graham cracker rim. (Ian considers a cocktail a first course.) The chocolate showed up in a Mexican mole sauce for chicken (not, as I had assumed, in my cookies). The brie was baked and served with sliced pears as an appetizer, which now seems altogether too obvious, but we needed one ace in the hole. And dessert was a homemade pear sorbet, which we made with store-bought pear juice in an ice cream maker that until then had been gathering frost in our freezer.

For that first dinner, Ian did most of the menu planning, and I just helped execute the meal (in a good way, not in an "I killed it" way, like I did with the London broil).

But just as I started to get into it with these dinners, Ian started to get out of it. This might be because I'm a perfectionist (or "bossy," as he might say), but eventually, it seemed like the division of labor became: Ian does the inviting, and I do everything else. Until the day of, when together we dice, slice, and cook for twelve hours straight—me running around like a game show contestant, Ian using every pot, pan, and gadget we own to make things I still find too complicated (like soufflés, rack of lamb, homemade pasta, salt-baked fish), often improvising items we did *not* discuss, like four giant homemade raviolis stuffed with lobster instead of little individual ones (not completely successful, but Ian was still pleased with the originality of it)—and suddenly the guests show up, at which point I realize I didn't leave time to shower, and Ian quickly serves drinks and is the perfect host as I smile and pretend to listen to their stories of the day (which was the point!) while simultaneously rereading the recipe for spring pea risotto with lemon and mint or whatever else I have over-ambitiously put on the menu.

And I'm talking about actual menus—my idea—because when I took over menu planning, although I hadn't cooked a lot, I'd dined out a lot, so I knew about menus. I knew when a meal sounded delicious, when you could taste every dish just by reading its description, when a chef's tasting menu enabled you to imagine the flow from amuse-bouche to dessert. And about the "amuse-bouche": once I started cooking, I found myself thinking, at restaurants, *I could put some sushi-grade tuna on a potato chip. We have a meat slicer; I could make the potato chips.* I began to realize I could make almost anything once I found a recipe, and I could even *vary* the recipe. I was becoming fearless, at least when it came to menu planning. So I started the tradition of printing menus for each of these dinners, which raised the bar and the stakes, because you can't nix a course once it's in print.

But I have never become fearless about failure. Ian always says, "Who cares? If a dish fails, we'll order a pizza."

But what if the dish that fails is a pizza? I wanted to know. And what if we're making that pizza for someone like Stanley Tucci? (I was working with Stanley Tucci at the time, but, of course, it was Ian who offered up a four-ingredient dinner.) Just as a reminder, Stanley Tucci co-wrote and co-directed *The Big Night*, a movie that was a celebration of Italian cooking based on his family's recipes, recipes that were not on a

bag of chocolate chips but have been published in the beautiful, full-color *The Tucci Cookbook* (which had originally
been published as *Cucina & Famiglia*—that's how authenti-
cally Italian these recipes were), and I promised, on the
printed menu, a pizza from said cookbook. I can't even blame
Ian for that. It was my idea, for some reason, to make a pizza
using Stanley Tucci's grandmother's recipe for pizza dough!
And as he politely examined the elasticity of the dough, I
thought, *I only just learned how to cook! Why am I compet-
ing over pizza with Stanley Tucci's Italian grandmother?*

But then this lovely man (Stanley Tucci, not Ian) showed
me how to transfer the pizza onto a pizza stone—that stone
being another item from our registry that I never thought
we'd use—and there I was (me, who was once afraid to make
biscuits without Bisquick!) making a prosciutto, goat cheese,
and arugula pizza from scratch, drizzled with aged balsamic,
for one of my favorite actor/writer/directors, and we all
agreed it could not have been more delicious. It was a fun,
luscious Big Night, and I felt as if I was graduating from
something, maybe from fear.

Step Five: Vodka. Did I mention the vodka? Vodka is helpful because it lessens my need for perfection, along with our
guests'. After Ian came up with the idea of a liquid first
course, our guests' ingredients starting making their way into
vodka infusions. And now, with at least four infusions going
at any one time, even if a meal is a disaster, nobody com-
plains. Or drives home, for that matter. My discovery: if it
would make a good ice cream or sorbet (blood orange, apple/

cinnamon, candied pumpkin, fresh fig), it would make a good vodka. Ian's discovery: tasting our infusions every night to see when they're perfectly ready does not make for a better vodka; it makes for a drunk husband. We finally agreed that it might be healthier for him to stop "testing" the vodkas and leave that to our guests, especially since Ian never felt the need to pretest anything else we served our guests (e.g., giant lobster raviolis). We had some failures (cherry vodka tasted like cough syrup; pizza-flavored vodka—another off-book idea of Ian's—tasted like oregano and tomato gone bad), but my candied pumpkin vodka (which is a labor of love) tasted like a labor of love, and became our signature vodka, which Ian begs me to make every fall. Vodka also helps when dinner is late, which ours inevitably is, because Ian likes to involve guests in the cooking, so the meal, by design, *can't* be ready when guests arrive.

Step Six: Involve Guests. I used to think letting friends help with the cooking meant asking someone to chop celery for the salad, but Ian will hand a guest a recipe for fish wrapped in banana leaves along with some banana leaves and wish them good luck. This might seem rude. It might *be* rude. But our friends have enjoyed the challenges we've thrown at them, like filling tamales or shaping their own homemade pasta. It lets them take pride in the meal, and helps me not panic (as much) when guests arrive and we're still frying Brussels sprout leaves for the rosemary sea-salt Brussels sprout crisps that I put on the menu as an appetizer.

Every so often I will catch Ian's eye and make it clear that something is not coming out as planned, and he will come kiss me and show me that it's not so bad—it just needs lemon, more garlic, more hands—and he will take over, or put someone else in charge, and somehow it all works out. These dinners always feel completely disorganized to me, which is something I will never get used to, but Ian loves the chaos of people cooking together. He doesn't even see it as chaos. He has no problem rushing out for more groceries ten minutes before everyone arrives, because he trusts that those groceries will turn into a beautiful dish with a little teamwork. And he's right. It's like a magic trick (a magic trick that takes several hours to clean up, but that's another chapter). Maybe we eat at 10 P.M., but as a novice chef, every time a meal turns out, I feel as if we pulled a rabbit out of a hat. And ate it. And it was delicious.

Step Seven: Involve Professionals. Ian and I decided it's not cheating to buy a course or two. In fact, it can be fun (albeit expensive) to include the world's best crab cakes flown in fresh from Baltimore if a guest chooses crab as one of her ingredients, or even if she hasn't. It's sometimes comforting to know that at least one course will be edible and worry-free, so we have flown in Faidley's crab cakes, Eileen's cheesecakes, Varsano's chocolates, Lobel's steaks, and my mom's cookies (she makes more than just Toll House cookies, and they're always crowd-pleasers).

Step Eight: Enjoy. This, for me, might be the hardest part, to relax and "enjoy" the evening when I know there are still four courses that need our attention, but I do find that if we invite only two to four people, instead of eight (which seems to be Ian's minimum), I have a shot at enjoying the dinner as much as our guests. I love when a group is small enough to have one conversation; otherwise, it always seems that giant bursts of laughter are coming from the end of the table where I am not. A small group means the cooking is more manageable, and you don't miss any laughs. And there are always plenty, because this is a long, luxurious, many-course night, and it does seem that when you share your home, people seem more comfortable sharing their stories.

And these are stories I have not heard!

So, once the dinner is under way, whether it's working or not, I try (which is also a process) to be in the moment and enjoy. I try to let the dishes pile up. I try to let the time between courses lag. I try to take in what is happening, because it is still astounding to me the meals and the friendships we have made.

We've invited couples we didn't know so well who have become great friends. We've cooked for houseguests, like my best friend from college and her husband (who chose rhubarb, not because he wanted to make life difficult, but because his mother makes a killer rhubarb crisp, and now I love cooking with rhubarb). I included a colleague who later became one of my dearest friends, Padma (Atluri, not Lakshmi), because she happened to mention she loved pumpkin when we were already planning a dinner that featured pumpkin (the birth of my famous pumpkin vodka). So sometimes the ingredients dictate the guest list, and sometimes the person who picks the ingredients dictates the guest list by bringing a few friends along for the treat. Once we invited four friends and let each pick one ingredient.

Surrendering control of everything from the ingredients to the guest list, trusting other people's choices, trusting Ian that the night will work out . . . I have to admit, it's all been good for me. Not easy. But good. Before marrying Ian, I never would have tried to update Peking duck (it's an ancient recipe!), but our roasted duck with farmers' market scallions and homemade thyme pancakes with pomegranate reduction was one of the most delicious dishes I have had anywhere, and I had it in my living room.

I guess the old me did operate from fear when it came to entertaining. I would buy food in advance. I would try to visualize how everyone would get along, try to bulletproof the evening. But just as I've learned that any four ingredients can be the basis of a great meal, I've learned that we can enjoy any combination of the people we love, because if each guest is special and amazing to us, by dessert they'll find one another just as special and amazing.

These elaborate menus we've attempted, these culinary leaps of faith—they've forced me to get out of my comfort zone, to fail at times and understand that it will be okay, to be surprised by what Ian and I can do as a team, and to marvel at what I can do as an individual within that team. So my extreme sport of choice is, in fact, a team sport. And maybe it's just one event in the grueling Olympic team sport that is marriage.

I can report, with confidence, that Ian and I have both grown from these dinners. In size. Apparently, we can't eat unlimited amounts of food without gaining weight. I'm glad Ian loves me at various weights (so far), and I love him at various weights, but we've had to scale back our dinner parties thanks to our scale, and we're trying to eliminate a few courses from our own daily diet.

At the moment, we're down to just dessert and vodka.

I Find My Husband Rappelling

I wish I could say that all wives experience this at one time or another, but I fear it's just me. I have been watching Ian literally rappelling down the side of a building with a garden hose wrapped around his waist.

It's actually kind of impressive.

It would be more impressive if Ian were not the one who had locked us out of Jason and Meredith's apartment in the first place, leaving the four of us stranded on their roof deck with a bottle of wine and the new baby we'd come to see. But luckily, this was not the first time I found Ian rappelling.

Ian and I learned to rappel on a waterfall in Costa Rica. It was part of a mom-and-pop zip-line tour run by the family who owned the land, designed the course, and even met us at the Turrialba bus station in their pickup truck.

I support mom-and-pop shops, but the jury is still out on mom-and-pop adventure travel. I know we're a litigious society here in America, but once you're in the back of a stranger's truck surrounded by harnesses and ropes, you might begin to wonder if the threat of lawsuits and the ubiquitous waivers and safety regulations and warnings and roped-off danger areas are maybe a good thing. I also began to wonder why the hell I agreed to do this. I wasn't eighteen anymore.

Oh, yeah, that's why I agreed to do it.

I was still single at the time, and being single in your late thirties means you have to do some seriously stupid shit to prove you're still fun, like ride in the back of a pickup, rappel down a waterfall, or go on a two-day river-rafting/camping trip, which Ian scheduled for after we rappelled down a waterfall.

Clearly, Costa Rica was an early trip for us. In fact, it was a trip Ian had planned before he met me, and he told me repeatedly (in addition to the fact that he was not looking for a relationship) that he would be going to Central America for a few months, and I shouldn't try to stop him.

I, in fact, had no intention of stopping him. I'm not sure what kind of controlling women he'd been with in the past, but I like to travel alone sometimes, and I respected the fact that he did, too.

Then, a few weeks before his departure, he sheepishly asked if I wanted to join him in Costa Rica. And that was our courtship in a nutshell. Ian would firmly announce whatever he was absolutely *not* going to do (have an exclusive relationship, or say "I love you" very often) and then would do the opposite. He still says "I love you" almost every day, and to the best of my knowledge we are still exclusive. I think he preferred to start with establishing low or no expectations so he could be happily surprising instead of sorely disappointing, which was a good strategy, because I usually started with unreasonably high expectations and had nowhere to go but down. Much like being at the top of a waterfall.

In Costa Rica our relationship literally got off the ground when we did this zip-line tour, because Ian was impressed that I was so game for everything. He started the trip alone with a Spanish immersion course, and I flew to Costa Rica to meet him, which, after I landed, involved driving two hours in a car with no A/C on a road that every so often was cut off by a body of water that my Spanish-only-speaking driver would nonchalantly drive through. I met Ian's host family and drank the lemonade I was offered (even though I'd been told absolutely not to drink the water), because I didn't want to insult them, and before I knew it, I was in a pickup truck headed for a family-owned ropes course.

I was *quite* game, come to think of it, and oddly good at rappelling, especially considering that I missed part of the safety briefing when I got distracted.

Our guide was wearing a harness as he spoke, and the harness fits around your thighs and cinches up around your shoulders, so if you are a tan man wearing shorts, which he was, it basically lifts and accentuates your penis. I don't think that's intentional, but this guy helped design the course, so you be the judge.

He was saying something to the effect of "This is very important: when you lean back, don't—" which is when I got distracted. Frankly, I think tan, muscular Latin men should not wear a harness when giving a safety lecture to women. I thought my momentary lapse went undetected, but that night at dinner, Ian said, "Were you checking out our guide's package?" and I did a spit take, an actual spit take with liquid spewing out of my mouth, which we laugh about to this day.

Ian, being straight (as opposed to other men I have married), was not distracted during the instructions, which is why he came up with the idea of wrapping a garden hose around his waist years later when we were trapped on a roof deck, as our friends and their baby stared in awe.

Let me add that it was not so awesome at first, when Ian flung himself over the railing without the aid of a garden hose and tried to balance on a sconce, from which he planned to jump to our friends' balcony below. The sconce immediately fell off the wall, which left Ian clinging to the edge of the roof like an action hero, except he wasn't an action hero, so it occurred to me that this might be how our relationship was going to end, with Ian hanging there until his fingers slipped, and then I would have to replace a husband and a sconce.

We managed to pull him back up, but he remained on what I will call "the wrong side of the railing." Then he spotted the garden hose on the roof deck behind us, wrapped around a large spindle, and he yelled, "Hand me the hose!" and we all told him to stop, it was too dangerous, but he looked me in the eyes with confidence, and repeated the order, *"Hand me the hose."*

I did what he asked, and as he looped the hose around his waist, I told him I loved him, but this was stupid. (I thought

it might be my last chance to say the words "This is stupid.")
Then, making sure there was no slack in the hose, and using
the railing for leverage, Ian planted his feet flat on the side of
the building and started to lean back. That's when I finally
realized what he was doing and said, "Oh, like the waterfall!"
And he smiled and proceeded to walk down the side of the
apartment as we fed him the hose, just as we had walked
down a waterfall, except there was no guide, no safety harness, and no real reason to do it.

Somewhere a landlord had a key to the apartment, but Ian
was on a mission.

So we didn't ask anyone in the small crowd that was form-
ing below to call the landlord or a locksmith. Instead we
watched and then applauded as Ian dropped down to the balcony, opened the sliding glass door, walked through the apartment, unlocked the door he had accidentally locked, went up
the stairs to the roof deck, and rescued us and the baby.

Jason claims he decided then and there that Ian would be
his law partner, and they still have a boutique firm together
today. Ian had passed the test.

And I had passed the "travel test" early on, when I went to
Central America with Ian. I did several things on that trip
that were out of my comfort zone in addition to rappelling
down a waterfall—like traveling without any real itinerary;
carrying a backpack instead of a suitcase; going without
showering; showering without hot water; hiking for ten hours
in one day, only to do it again the next day, and the next, and
the next to get to Machu Picchu at sunrise; staying with a

local family in Lake Titicaca and dressing up in native garb to dance (despite the high altitude, which made dancing challenging even if you weren't cinched into a native dress); spending a night on a bus, and using the bus bathroom, which was clearly visible from the street when the bus stopped—and, of course, the bus stopped just at the moment that I had finally worked up the nerve to enter said bathroom, so I was on view, hovering above the tin hole that was the toilet, for all of the elderly Peruvians boarding the bus to see. That was *certainly* out of my comfort zone. And theirs.

Ian did things that were out of his comfort zone, too, like staying a few nights at the Four Seasons Resort Costa Rica at Peninsula Papagayo, which I had arranged like an oasis of hot food (and hot water) in the middle of our trip. For Ian, staying at a Four Seasons was akin to voting Republican. He couldn't even tell his friends he was doing it. (Years later, at the Amansomethingorother, Ian would be the one on the phone to the concierge, complaining that we didn't get turndown service and that our minibar needed refilling, but this was early in our travels together, and we were still getting used to each other's lifestyle.)

The thing about passing a travel test in a relationship is that all it really means is that you've graduated to the next trip, where you will be given a different travel test. For example, no sooner had I passed my Central American test and established myself firmly as Ian's girlfriend than I had to start training for the international competition that was being held in the south of France.

We had been invited by Ian's best (and frankly, most

beautiful) friends, Philippe and Amy, to celebrate Philippe's fortieth birthday at his family's sprawling summer home in the south of France. We would be joining their fabulous international friends, eating delicious French food, and swimming at the gorgeous French Riviera, and I was dreading it, because Ian said there was talk of a surprise Amy was planning for Philippe's birthday, a show or performance of some kind, and all the women would be participating, me included, and we might be topless.

Excuse me, *what*?

The details were vague, and as I was getting them through Ian, I never got anything like the full picture, but the partial picture was enough to start giving me anxiety about the trip. I asked Ian to tell Amy that if the women would be doing a topless "can-can," his girlfriend "can't-can't," but we were still very much looking forward to the trip.

He said, "Let's just go and see what it is," which I took to mean that he didn't want to seem uncool (like his girlfriend was uncool) to these people, his coolest of cool friends.

The details continued to be slow in coming even once we got to France. We were all much too busy enjoying the food, wine, cheese, bread, beach, pool, and view, but I never stopped secretly dreading the "show."

I finally learned that it wasn't a show, it was a *tableau vivant*, which is a live reenactment of a painting. I don't know if there was an actual painting we were reenacting—if there was, I never saw it—but I gathered there would be topless women at the center of it, fanned out like a flower.

I finally worked up the nerve to tell Amy that although I was so appreciative to be included in the festivities, I really didn't feel comfortable being topless. And that is when Amy assured me that I wasn't supposed to be—I was going to be in a toga serving grapes or reading books or something equally benign on the fringes of the "painting," while she and her friends who had been models like her (did I mention she had been a model?) would be topless.

I was torn between being insulted and relieved. It was like breaking up with someone who didn't know he was dating you. But there was no time to be embarrassed. The men were already sequestered inside the house, and the women were scurrying around the grounds, spreading out flowers, preparing to become a living painting that may or may not have existed in real life.

The models stripped down to their G-strings and sprayed themselves with gold paint as nonchalantly as if they did this every day. I was given a sheet with which to fashion a toga, and I was told I could put it on over my sundress, making me feel like the least naked person in the south of France. And then I was spray-painted gold—maybe as a consolation prize—and given a book of poetry and positioned to look as if I was reading to my friend Liz, and she was finding the whole thing (and my nervousness) hilarious, which worked for her character, because she was supposed to be midlaugh, enjoying the poetry I was reading to her, as our friend Christina (also in toga) stood by holding a ceramic pitcher.

Finally Amy announced that we were ready, and we all

held perfectly still for five minutes as the men (and Philippe's parents!) viewed us from the house's wraparound porch. I am told it was quite breathtaking from above. I felt silly, not because I was in a toga spray-painted gold, but because I had wasted so much time and energy worrying about this *tableau vivant* when there was so much more to worry about.

There was all-night dancing (in clubs and at the summer house), techno music (in clubs and at the summer house), chicken fights in the pool (and even though Ian was game for chicken fighting, I really didn't see the victory in pushing a ninety-pound model off someone's shoulders), so the whole trip seemed to accentuate my not-comfortable-being-nakedness, physically and emotionally. And although Ian always loves me and my body, he doesn't love when my feelings about my body keep me (and us) from having fun. So I have to concede that my rampant insecurities caused me to fail the South of France test, but I was determined to improve in the future. I would try, on future trips, to do as Ian does: just go and see what it is.

That's how I found myself at a Ping-Pong show in Thailand.

Ian and I were married at that point, and Thailand was a "last hurrah" trip. It wasn't our first last hurrah, and it wouldn't be our last, but as our baby quest became more science project than sex, we used travel as a consolation prize when things didn't work out, and as a last hurrah even if they only seemed like they might, because we'd been cleared for yet another round of IVF. Subsequently we spent a lot of money on travel.

In Chiang Mai we had a Valentine's Day date that was as

over-the-top glamorous as something you'd see on *The Bachelor*. It's sad that my idea of romance is now shaped by *The Bachelor*, but this night in Chiang Mai was truly television-worthy. We were led down a paper lantern–lit path to a private gazebo overlooking the rice paddies; musicians serenaded us with Thai music; we had a delicious five-course meal; and afterward we lit a candle that launched a traditional rice paper hot-air balloon into the starry sky, sending to the heavens a wish we no longer had to say aloud.

There was, however, one wish Ian did say aloud on our last night in Thailand, and it was one of the least romantic things he's ever proposed: he wanted us to see a sex show in Patpong.

I didn't know what that entailed, but I did know that (1) I did not wish to see strangers having sex, (2) I did not wish to have sex in front of strangers, and (3) I did not wish animals to be involved in any way.

Ian assured me that the show would not include sex acts or animal acts, and that it was known among tourists as a Ping-Pong show.

Now my curiosity was piqued, not just because I'm a good Ping-Pong player (although I have to say, "Ping-Pong in Patpong" had a certain poetry I found hard to resist), but also because as a woman you hear tales of bachelor parties where strippers shoot Ping-Pong balls or eggs or strawberries out of their hoohahs. (Well, *I* hear those stories. Maybe other women don't, but I always press men for details without any sign of being judgmental, because men don't give you details when you're judging.) So I figured this might be my only chance to see a woman shoot a Ping-Pong ball out of her hoohah.

Plus, cards on the table, I had never been to a strip club with Ian or any other guy.

I know, it's shocking. Most of the women I think are cool (and even some I do not) have gone on a strip club date at least once. This is not a date you will see on *The Bachelor*, incidentally, but my friends have reported either watching a boyfriend get a lap dance, getting one themselves for his amusement, or getting one for their own amusement. Any of those options seemed to require more alcohol than I was currently drinking, but a sex show in Bangkok would certainly clear up any unexplained gaps in my sexual résumé. At least, that's what I was thinking when we told our cabdriver we were going to Patpong.

He grinned and said, "Ping-Pong show?" We nodded. He laughed. I'm still not sure if he was laughing with us or at us. I figured Patpong was a tourist trap, the kind of place no locals would bother going. Or maybe there were more authentic, traditional Ping-Pong shows that the locals preferred. In fact, what our cabdriver was probably thinking was *We've got ancient temples, rich cultural traditions, beautiful landscapes, and these bozos want to see a girl popping Ping-Pong balls out of her vagina.*

Yeah, in retrospect, I'm pretty sure he was laughing *at* us.

Just as you get handed a menu outside some restaurants in foreign countries, a similar bill of fare was available outside of sex shows in Patpong.

I felt for the women holding these laminated menus, setting aside for the moment the reason they were laminated. I feared the menu holders were deemed not pretty enough to be *in* the sex show, so each was in khaki pants and a solid-color golf shirt that matched the solid-color bikinis of the girls in their club. Through the open doorway you could see the girls inside, listlessly dancing on a stage in bikinis and go-go boots, some in athletic socks and sneakers. But outside, their Ping-Pong protégées were enthusiastically handing us a menu and waving us in.

The menu made it clear that sluggish dancing was just an amuse-bouche, because typed in English was a list of what we could expect to see, including but not limited to:

Pussy Plays Ping-Pong
Pussy Smokes a Cigarette
Pussy Blows a Whistle
Pussy Drinks a Soda
Pussy Writes a Letter

Everything sounded impressive, but I was most intrigued by "Pussy Writes a Letter." Maybe it was the writer in me, but I couldn't help but wonder (thank you, Carrie Bradshaw): *To whom was this pussy writing, and what did the letter say?* I told Ian we had to see Pussy Writes a Letter, and he agreed and promptly paid the cover charge, and in we went.

It was a slow night in Patpong, so after we were seated in this smallish, dimly lit theater in the round, we were immediately surrounded by dancers, some now topless but still in socks and sneakers, some who spoke a little English (which made the whole thing more awkward rather than less). They giggled and prodded Ian to kiss me, and then they wanted to kiss us, and then, I'm not sure, but I think there was a back room involved.

We tried to explain we were just there for Pussy Writes a Letter, as if we had come for a Broadway matinee and they were talking over the orchestra. They didn't seem to care.

Frankly, Pussy was a little pushy, so we left, and at the next club, Ian paid more than the cover charge to ensure that we not be bothered. We were given a large red balloon (which I figured was code for *Please don't try to have sex with these people*) but as soon as we sat down, there was a loud *pop* and I realized a blow dart had been shot directly into our balloon from the stage, where a dancer was pointing her crotch at us.

She put on her bikini bottoms and came down to collect the remains of the balloon and her tip, and that was the first sign that we would be spending and doing much more *not* to have sex than we would spend and do to have it. You see, other than a drunk guy who looked rather creepy, we were again the only tourists there, which meant we had front-row seats, which you don't necessarily want for this particular show. It was like having front-row seats for a birth.

And we were basically expected to applaud heartily and assist in all the tricks.

I'm not proud of this, but I did everything from lighting a cigarette (Pussy Blows Smoke Rings!) to returning a Ping-Pong ball. My view for the former was disturbingly good, but

I couldn't look away, because then Pussy Catches Fire. As far as returning the Ping-Pong ball, okay, maybe I *am* a little proud of that. I don't know how many participants actually return the ball with the paddle you're given, but I did, and the fact that Ian cheered for me instead of for the naked woman onstage made me happy I married him.

Incidentally, Pussy put olive oil—or some kind of oil—on the Ping-Pong balls, which I thought was sort of cheating. I mean, what wouldn't come flying out of your vagina if you covered it in olive oil?

As I pondered that question, Ian was pulling on the end of a brightly colored handkerchief that led to another brightly colored handkerchief, and another, and another. You might have seen this trick performed by a clown or magician, but when Pussy did it, frankly, it wasn't so impressive. I mean, you knew where the handkerchiefs were coming from, and you didn't really want to think about it.

Pussy Sips a Soda was probably the ickiest trick. The dancer put a soda bottle between her legs and then did a handstand, emptying the contents of the bottle into herself; then she got upright and moved her hips for a while, then reinserted the bottle and filled it up again. She offered the refilled bottle to us, and we tipped her almost everything we had left to take it away.

Pussy Uses Chopsticks really made me question what my own pussy had done for me lately. Of all the acts we saw that night, that one seemed to require the most skill. I can barely manage chopsticks using my fingers.

I started to think about who originated these tricks. Did word filter down the street that a dancer at Thai-One-On (not a real place, but should be) had put chopsticks on the menu, and then all the dancers scrambled to get it on their club's menu, much like what happened in California with quinoa? Furthermore, if I can do Kegel exercises, could I learn to manipulate chopsticks? Forget the human brain; apparently we're only using 10 percent of our vaginas.

The fact that my mind was wandering made me realize something else rather remarkable: I was bored. These pussies were working their asses off (if that's possible) and I was sort of feeling *Seen one pussy blow out birthday candles, seen them all.*

So Ian went to the bar and asked how long before Pussy Writes a Letter, because we weren't leaving until we saw that. The bartender made a note and passed it to a dancer, and she dutifully went onstage, took off her bikini bottoms, put a felt-tipped marker in her vagina, and squatted over a large piece of paper, all the time referring to the note from the bartender until she had gyrated and produced a sign that said, "Hello Cindy Ian!"

As we rode home, rolled-up letter in hand, my attempt to salvage the night with some fun, colorful local transportation ended with a crash, literally, when our *tuk tuk* (bicycle rickshaw) collided with a slow-moving car. Ian and I barely spoke as we left the *tuk tuk* and got into a regular taxi.

I felt vaguely depressed. I'd like to say it was the fact that we had witnessed the exploitation of young girls, but honestly, they didn't seem to mind. It felt more as if they were exploiting *us*. (Cue angry letters, some written by Pussy.) But what I mean is, it seemed as if they had been showing off. There, I said it. My pussy couldn't even muster the most basic trick—Pussy Produces a Person—and theirs were sipping sodas.

I felt that what Pussy really wanted to write in her letter was: "I'm a pussy. I should be having fun. So why do I feel like I'm working?"

But maybe I was projecting.

And maybe Ian was projecting that night at Jason and Meredith's when he decided we needed a hero to rescue us from the roof deck. More likely, Ian needed to feel like a rock star (or at least a rock climber) after congratulating yet another couple on yet another child while we were still nowhere near getting one of our own.

But for me, both of those nights—the night Ian rappelled down the side of an apartment building and the night he applauded my Ping-Pong playing at a Thai Ping-Pong show— were about what a great match we were.

Some people get boring when they get married. I used to worry that marriage meant my life would get smaller and more predictable, but with Ian, the opposite is true. I think it bodes well for our future that after all of these years, I still find my husband rappelling.

For Richer, for Poorer

Most couples don't think of a prenup as a romantic moment in their relationship, but in our case, it was. Ian insisted on an agreement that made it crystal clear that he was not marrying me for my money, and that I would not inherit his many debts, and that if the marriage ended, he would basically leave with the shirt on his back. Even the pants, I believe, were at my discretion.

My accountant, a woman usually wary of men who marry "up," said that even she would not advise Ian to sign such a document, let alone propose it, but he ignored her advice, and she has heartily approved of him ever since.

Ian is secure enough in his manhood to be comfortable making less money than his wife. "I'm very comfortable with it," he jokes (a joke I'm slightly uncomfortable with).

He's always been extremely grateful that my success (doing something I love, I should add) has enabled him to do the kind of legal work he loves and finds meaningful—even though meaningless, soul-killing jobs (like the one he had when I met him) pay better.

After marrying me, Ian spent several years working for the Public Defender's office, representing people who couldn't afford representation, and he also did pro bono work in conjunction with the Center for Constitutional Rights, representing Guantanamo Bay detainees. I am proud of the work Ian does, and of the integrity and heart he puts into it, and I often tell friends "the currency of happiness" is just as valuable as actual money in a relationship.

But I might be full of shit, because sometimes I catch myself thinking things I am reluctant to admit, like that I should have more say in our relationship because I make more money.

Don't judge me.

Most days I don't even think about who makes what. We're a team. The fact that I put more into the team's joint bank account because my teammate could not live three months on what he makes never crosses my mind.

Okay, maybe it does. But when the issue really bubbles up is when Ian says things like someday he'd like to build a cabin in the woods where he could keep a horse.

That's a very romantic image, but instead I'm thinking *I'm not buying you a horse*. And he's not, in fact, asking me to buy him that horse. But I don't see his being able to afford a horse, let alone building the cabin where he's going to keep the horse, so I have moments when I think those thoughts, and then I feel horrible, like I do right now.

Let me give you another example, one that doesn't make Ian sound like such a dreamy pioneer horse whisperer.

One day in the car, we were talking about the fact that we weren't having sex that often.

Yes, it's true. Even though when I was single I used to get all up in my stuff and say, "Show me a woman who doesn't want to have sex with her husband, and I will show you a man who doesn't know how to kiss her!" I was wrong. I now understand, especially if infertility is part of the equation, that there are times, even if you're married to a very good kisser, when you won't be excited about sex—and with any luck you won't be responsible for a sex column for O, *The Oprah Magazine*, when that happens, and they won't put a tagline by your photo that says, "Have no sexual fear, Cindy Chupack is here!"

Probably because of that damn column, I took this opportunity to open up a dialogue with Ian about what might make sex more fun for each of us again, and I listed a few ideas— nothing crazy, just things like switching up the position more often; trying to have sex before dinner instead of after so we wouldn't be too tired or too full. (That's an issue that comes up only once you marry, by the way. I don't remember ever choosing side dishes over sex when I was single, and yet now, a really delicious creamed spinach or lobster mac and cheese seems worth taking another night off.)

Ian nodded thoughtfully and started to add something, but then decided against it.

Being a sex columnist, a "sexpert," I did what I would

advise readers to do: I told my husband there was nothing we shouldn't be able to say to each other.

Turns out that is the biggest lie of all.

There are plenty of things married people should never say to each other, and Ian was about to say one of them: "I've been thinking maybe you might like to get a breast reduction."

My jaw dropped. Just like my boobs had, apparently.

I didn't see how that was relevant. Yes, I have big(gish) boobs, but I've always had them. I used to wish they were smaller, but they grew on me. I mean literally, they grew on me, so I can't imagine abandoning them.

And supposedly Ian liked big boobs. He always told me the story of how he once was at a Billy Idol concert with a female friend, and as they were dancing to "Rebel Yell" he got distracted by her cleavage and decided then and there that he was a boob man. What was the point of that story if not to attest to the fact that he liked a nice rack, particularly mine? It's not a great story to tell your wife otherwise.

"What's the big deal?" he asked. "All of your friends have done it." I couldn't think of one, and he proceeded to name several of my friends—all of whom, in fact, had had breast cancer.

"A double mastectomy is *not* a boob job," I said, dumbfounded. "It's not elective surgery if it's potentially lifesaving."

"Still," he went on, slightly deflated (as he was hoping *I* might be someday): "They seem happy with their new boobs."

I was starting to rethink the boob I married.

"And a lot of women do it after they have children," he

continued, as if his suggestion might still be welcome, even appreciated.

I reminded him that we hadn't had children yet, and the way things were going I might never give birth or nurse, so my breasts might not be adversely affected.

He seemed relieved, which just made me more annoyed. "How is any of this relevant to our sex life?" I asked.

"I just thought you might enjoy sex more if they were smaller," he said.

I never thought of my boobs getting in the way of sex. They're not so big that they're actually obscuring things, if that's what you're wondering. And to be honest, they've never been a particularly erotic zone for me. I've always wanted to tell men to move along when they get hung up there.

Ian finally explained the sex might be better . . . for him. He might want it more if I had smaller boobs. He said, maybe a little sheepishly, that he'd been noticing smaller boobs lately. . . .

By now even Ian could see this was not a good tact.

"I wouldn't ask you to get a penis enlargement," I said, after contemplating this unexpected new turn in our relationship.

He asked if I wanted him to.

He knew I didn't want him to. His penis is fine. Perfect, actually. (Ian made me add that line.)

Anyhow, I should have said, "Yes, I've been noticing bigger penises lately," just to be tit for tat, so to speak.

We drove in silence for a while, which is what we should have done from the beginning, and then I had a thought I did not say aloud or even admit thinking until just now: *You don't make enough money to ask me to get a boob job.*

I was shocked that that had even occurred to me, but then again, it did seem true. Rich men can ask their trophy wives to do anything, they can dress them how they want, they can make their boobs as big or small as they want, they can even complain about how much their wives spend, and somehow it all seems like bragging instead of complaining. It's all fine if you bring home the bacon.

Bring home the Bacon Bits, and I control my tits.

(I didn't say that aloud either, but I was tempted to, on account of the rhyme and all.)

So there it was—the horrible, awful truth about how a woman (me) might feel when she makes more money than her husband. There might be strings attached that she didn't even know were there until he tugged on the wrong one, specifically one that would require her to go under the knife. I'm not a plastic surgery kind of person. I'm probably the only Jewish woman in the world who has had two deviated septum operations and no nose job.

So where does this leave women? I'm certain we haven't worked as hard as we have to break the glass ceiling only to wish the men in our lives made more money. I know I was lucky to be able to choose the man I wanted to marry instead of the man I needed to marry.

To my credit (or detriment), I was never one of those women who were looking for a rich husband. (A) I weigh more than 108 pounds, and (B) I find the "gold digger" stereotype offensive. I don't really know women whose main criterion for a partner is wealth. I know they exist (because I have seen *The Millionaire Matchmaker*), but most of my female friends and colleagues are more than capable of earning their own way.

The truth is, I like being self-sufficient. I remember how good it felt, at sixteen, to be able to buy an expensive chunky sweater with my waitressing tips. It was a sweater my parents never would have bought me (probably because it made my boobs look bigger).

As an adult, supporting myself had always meant having the freedom to leave an unhappy marriage. It never occurred to me that I might wind up in a happy marriage in which I was supporting someone else.

Then again, there are many forms of support (in addition to underwire bras), and Ian *does* support me in countless ways. He puts up with my moods. He roots for me at the right moments for the right reasons. (For example, he's especially proud when I stick to my guns creatively, because he knows that's not easy in Hollywood.) He comforts me and calms me when times are tough. He always believes in me, and I believe in him. I'm not convinced that, if it came to it, he *could* actually build a cabin in the woods, but I'm also not convinced that he won't convince me to let him try.

A marriage, for better or worse, takes you places you never dreamed of going, places *someone else* dreamed of going, and that annoyingly persistent other dreamer is your spouse.

I know these are luxury problems. I know I'm extremely

blessed, especially in this economy, to be able to do what I love, and to earn enough doing it so that my husband can do what he loves. I know I'm lucky to live with a man who cares more about making a difference than about making money (although he continues to try to do both), and I know I'm fortunate to live in a country where women have the same opportunity as men to resent their spouses.

Uch, even my boobs are a luxury problem. Boo-hoo, my boobs are too big.

Maybe I will get a breast reduction one day.

But not because Ian asked me to.

Because it will be easier to ride his horse with smaller breasts.

We're Having a Maybe!

'Twas the day after Christmas, and I was reading *News-week*'s cover story on diet and fertility when I stood up, ripped the roof off a gingerbread house, and ate it, like Godzilla.

This was not something the cover story recommended, by the way. It was, however, a reaction to something the cover story recommended—namely, that you shouldn't eat a lot of red meat if you were trying to get pregnant.

I was, as it happened, trying to get pregnant. I'd been trying for the past two and a half years. I also had a steak on the grill, a petite filet that was going to be my lunch before I decided to have the gingerbread house instead.

"Trying" is a good word for this process. At first, "trying" just meant sex without birth control, but when you marry at forty, "trying" quickly becomes more trying, and eventually Ian and I had enlisted the requisite army of experts, most of whom insurance didn't cover—but of course, you can't put a price on a baby.

You can put a price, though, on *not* having a baby. By now that was running us close to $45,000 in credit card debt.

So by the time I was reading that *Newsweek* article, I'd done it all . . . drugs, shots, suppositories, IUI, IVF, that test with the blue dye, acupuncture, stinky teas, human growth hormone injections. . . . Once, while we were driving to see a doctor in Beverly Hills, Ian asked what kind of doctor he was, and I said, "I don't know, but someone said to see him, so we're seeing him!" It was that doctor, incidentally, who told me to visualize my husband's face on a cartoon sperm with arms welcoming my egg to him. We decided the guy was a quack, so I saw him only two times a week for about four months.

The thing is, when you're racing your biological clock, people can tell you pretty much anything and you'll do it. At that point I was still worrying that I needed to track down some saint named Amachi so I could bring her red bananas. Recently a friend had said something about inversions— standing on your head. He hadn't been sure if you were supposed to do it before sex, during, or just in general, but the method had worked for two women he knew, so I figured I had to start standing on my head, too. I'd probably visualize Ian's face on a cartoon sperm while I was at it, not because I was on board with that. It was just a hard image to shake.

I did have limits, though. Several friends had highly recommended a fertility doctor in the Valley, but I would go to China for a baby before I'd go to the Valley.

We had become accustomed to paying people to tell us we weren't pregnant, so it was almost revolutionary that, for the holidays that year, we made the decision to return to the old-fashioned method of not getting pregnant on our own.

We went to Jackson Hole, and we didn't even take ovulation sticks, which might not seem crazy to you people, but when you're in the middle of this madness, not knowing when you're ovulating is like not knowing where your cell phone is.

And that was the idea. We wanted to lose ourselves for a while. We wanted to just have sex. Every day, you know, just in case, but even so, it was fun again, and that's how everyone had been saying that it finally worked for them, or for somebody they knew, or for somebody somebody they knew knew.

And in the weeks after that trip, I felt good. Well, *bad* good. I mean, my breasts were tender, I felt a little nauseous, I was dead tired . . . I had all the bad good signs of pregnancy, which I recognized, because I'd been pregnant before.

We actually got pregnant on our honeymoon, and for a moment we were some of the people I now call "those people" (people who got pregnant right away, maybe even accidentally, which now seems as likely to me as accidentally becoming invisible), but back then I didn't know any better, so we were "those people" until three months later, when we found out the baby's head was too large, and there was fluid where there shouldn't have been, and it had a malformed heart, and the baby would not make it to term.

The doctor said we should seriously consider termination unless we were deeply religious. That news was hard to take, but even harder because I felt guilty. The truth is, at that time, I didn't want to be pregnant.

We'd just gotten married. I still wasn't sure it was going to last. I also thought a few months as a couple would be nice, since it had taken us forty years to find each other.

But Ian was eager to start a family, so the morning after he proposed we were walking on the beach, and I threw my birth control pills into the ocean in a dramatic display of love and good faith, and it made him so happy that I had to resist the urge to run screaming into the surf to retrieve them.

I had always wanted to have a baby . . . in five years. I'd been saying I wanted to have a baby in five years for about the past twenty. I just had never felt ready.

But ready or not, we conceived on our wedding night, and on day seven of our honeymoon I felt nauseous and, thinking I had a stomach bug, I stayed in our room.

We were in South Africa on a safari, and they had warned us to keep the sliding doors to our bungalow locked because of the monkeys, but we hadn't seen any monkeys, and anyhow, I thought they meant we needed to keep the doors locked when we were out.

I was curled up in bed when all of a sudden I heard the door open, and I called out, thinking it was Ian. Then I heard a *thump thump thump thump* . . . and I knew something wasn't right, so I got up and looked into the living room, and there were *seven* monkeys throwing food around, and they froze as if I had just walked in on a teenager's party.

One was on a table by a big bowl of fruit, and it just stared at me, holding an apple, midbite. And the funny thing, looking back, was that this had been precisely my fear: this is what I thought it would be like to have children. This is why I never felt ready.

Cut to the day of the termination. We were already distraught, and then on the way to the appointment, we got pulled over by the police because Ian didn't see a woman walk into the crosswalk. I did see the woman, but she was on the other side of the street, plus I was trying not to say anything as Ian had taken to charging me five dollars every time I told him how to drive, but the policeman pulled us over and asked, "Are you trying to kill someone?!"

And I was thinking *Yes, that's exactly what we're trying to do, and if you would let us go, we could get on with it.*

I remember that, the rest of the way to the clinic, I was pissed at Ian for not having seen the woman, and he was pissed at the policeman for being such a dick, and the truth was, we were both just pissed at the universe for giving us this gift that we had to return.

But now, thanks to Jackson Hole, we were getting a second chance. And this time, when I took the pregnancy test, I was praying for a positive result rather than dreading it. But, of course, it was negative.

That was in the morning, and then a few hours later I was reading *Newsweek* and the next thing I knew, I was eating a gingerbread house.

The gingerbread itself was pretty hard. I think it had been made in Korea and not meant for eating, although that was never explicitly stated, just as it's not explicitly stated that you shouldn't eat candles. Some things you're just supposed to know. It came from a kit, one of six kits my friend had purchased for her annual gingerbread-house decorating party, so I had decorated alongside five women who were all mothers, some several times over, one with her newborn son in tow, and I knew it wasn't a competition, but my gingerbread house was the best.

Sure, these ladies had kids, but *I* had the Sistine Chapel of gingerbread houses. And I was proud of it, as sad as that might be. So just factor that in when you're imagining me eating it, like Godzilla. It was like eating my young, since, as we've established, there were no actual young.

I had decorated the roof with white icing, little sour balls, red Twizzlers, and green gumdrops, none of which tasted very good. What I really wanted was the door, which was made of Hershey's Special Dark chocolate.

Maybe you're wondering why I didn't just pull the door off. Well, I tried that, but the icing for these things is like glue, and the door was stuck to the front of the house, and the whole house was stuck to a foil-covered piece of cardboard, so you had to eat the roof before you could eat the door.

Well, you didn't have to eat the roof. You could, I suppose, just rip it off. But I was upset for all the reasons I've mentioned, and red meat was the final straw.

See, not only did I have a steak on the grill, I'd had a steak on the grill almost every day for the past year. Diet, for me, had been the most rewarding and punishing part of this baby quest. I'd gone from my highest weight ever to my lowest, because I didn't want to go from my highest to an even higher weight during pregnancy; that would mean spending the rest of my life in caftans. Given how many fears I had about what becoming a parent would do to my career and life (monkeys in the room!), I wanted to at least limit what it could do to my wardrobe. Plus it was supposed to be healthier to get pregnant at a healthier weight.

So I went on a supervised diet with someone we will just call Dr. Skinny. His office was powder blue with white molding, so that the whole thing looked like a Wedgwood plate. He was tall and thin (only 6 percent body fat! he would tell you), and he wore bad blue suits (from K-Mart! he would tell you) and I suspect he wore a toupee, but I was never able to confirm this, even though he confirmed your need to lose weight by pinching your sides with his fingers, so I should have just reached out and grabbed his hair one day in retaliation.

Dr. Skinny was basically an obesity doctor, so I was hoping that when I went to the first group meeting he sponsored that he and the group would say, "What are *you* doing here?" but instead, he snapped my "before" picture, and the next thing I knew, I was weighing my food at restaurants and doing lines of Splenda in the bathroom.

The Dr. Skinny diet is called an "eating plan," but it is really a "not eating plan." It definitely works, but it's very strict. You're not allowed a gingerbread house, that's for sure. It's basically protein and vegetables with Wasa crackers thrown in for survival. You get only two meals a day, with only three ounces of protein per meal, so I decided my protein would be filet mignon whenever possible.

My plan was to lose weight until I got pregnant, but since it was taking so long to get pregnant, I ate a lot of red meat, and I lost a lot of weight. Fifty pounds, to be exact.

For the first time ever, I felt like someone who belonged in Los Angeles. I bought a pair of skinny jeans and strutted my significantly smaller stuff down Robertson Boulevard. I felt, in a word, fabulous. So fabulous, in fact, that it took me a while to notice that I wasn't getting my period. And not for the reason I'd been hoping.

As annoying and depressing as it is to get your period each month when you're trying to get pregnant, it's nothing compared to *not* getting your period for five months when you're trying to get pregnant. So although I loved my skinny jeans, I didn't love them enough to give up having a baby, and I still don't think it's fair that that might be the price I'd have to pay for wearing them. I thought $178 was expensive. It's like I made a deal with the skinny devil.

I did get my period back, thanks to going off my "not eating plan," which I approached with the gusto of someone who's been told to gain weight for a role. And thanks, also, to Dr. Dao, who suggested "electro-acupuncture" to jumpstart my ovaries.

That was another mistake I'd made. I'd left Dr. Dao of "Mao and Dao" at the Tao of Wellness six months earlier. If you've ever tried to get pregnant in Los Angeles, someone has probably recommended going to them for acupuncture, and it's worth it, if only for the friendly desk staff, soothing music, heat lamps, and weekly nap. I loved Dr. Dao, but I saw him only once a month. For the other three visits each month I saw another doctor in the practice, who was very nice, but he didn't show after my first IVF attempt failed, and he didn't show again the following week, so not only was I forced to see someone who wasn't even Asian, I found out the reason my usual doctor hadn't appeared was that his wife had just had her second baby. Like I said, I know this wasn't a competition, but I was mildly annoyed that this nice man was sticking needles in me, and in all of these other women, listening patiently to our fertility problems, while at home, his wife was just pushing 'em out.

I'm not saying my decision was rational. I'm not saying it was pretty. But I did leave Dr. Dao for another acupuncturist and immediately regretted it, because she forgot every week why I was there, so I had to explain each time about how I hadn't had a period for two, then three, then four, then five months, and each time she reacted with horror. "Five months?!" And her receptionist was downright surly.

So I finally returned, contrite, to Dr. Dao, and he agreed we needed to jump-start my ovaries, which, I'm not kidding, involved tiny little spark plugs that were attached to the needles they put in my stomach and caused a *zap zap zap* sensation.

There was a control that changed the speed and intensity of the *zap zap zap*. And usually Dr. Dao would set the dial, but once he left me alone with it and let me control it, and that's when I wondered if maybe I was in some sort of cruel medical experiment in which they were trying to figure out how far a woman would go to have a baby. Would she stand on her head? Lose fifty pounds? Blow up her ovaries? Keep turning it up until . . . *poof*!

Because really, how much disappointment could one woman take? How many times could you be hopeful when odds were that you were going to get sucker punched by your period or a negative pregnancy test or something else you had never seen coming?

And yet you couldn't stress about that, because stress was the worst thing for fertility.

I knew, by the way, that once you had a baby, this all got put behind you. I knew the end of this movie. I didn't know where or when or how to get there. My fertility doctor broached the idea of donor eggs, but I didn't really like having guests in my house, so in my womb . . . I don't know.

But that was the point: You don't know. You don't know what dream you'll be willing to abandon and what dream you'll be willing to adopt. You only know that once you have your baby, the movie will be rewritten so that is the only possible ending, the only baby for you, but for now, you're just slogging your way through the second act.

Which you have to do, I guess. As in any worthwhile endeavor, you have to go through the hard, unsavory part before you get to the good stuff. You have to eat the roof before you can eat the door.

The Great Escape

Why do men get man caves, but women don't get dame dens? Are men really so oppressed in the company of women that they need somewhere to hibernate?

"Yes," said Ian. And he proceeded to design what he now fondly calls the Escape Pod.

At first I was annoyed by the name. What exactly was he escaping *from*? He smiled at me as if the answer was too obvious to say aloud. (Me. He was escaping from *me*.)

Rubber-stamping the Escape Pod was (a) probably part of the reason Ian wanted an Escape Pod in the first place, because why did everything in our marriage require my rubber stamp? and (b) my final attempt to cure Ian of his other mode of escape: pot.

I should clarify that Ian has a prescription for pot, which makes it legal in California, and he got his prescription from an OB/GYN, which should be an indication of what a racket this whole business has become. I think she prescribed it for insomnia. How staying up all night watching action movies and eating barbecued ribs is a cure for insomnia, I'm not sure, but maybe I'll understand more when we get the results of his pap smear.

Ian and I don't fight often, but when we do, it's almost always about his right to party. I have nothing against pot or pot smokers per se, but even other pot smokers will tell you that when Ian smokes pot, he doesn't become more fun. He becomes inanimate.

I once thought that maybe the problem wasn't the pot but the element of surprise. I never knew exactly whom I was coming home to: Ian or this other guy, his catatonic cousin. So, ever the creative problem solver, I suggested Friday High Day. That way Ian could partake once a week, and I could plan ahead to see friends, thereby avoiding his annoying cousin altogether.

Despite the catchy name, Friday High Day did not catch on. Ian felt one designated day a week was too limiting, and I thought it wasn't limiting enough. The way I figured it, if we were married seven years, I would have spent one entire year with Ian's catatonic cousin, who, by the way, I never would have married. I probably wouldn't even have become friends with him. He's lousy company.

I finally asked Ian if he could refrain from smoking pot just while we were trying IVF. I made this request *after* my first night of progesterone injections. I had already been nervous about the needle Ian was holding, which seemed much longer than necessary, when I noticed him staring a little too intently at the liquid in the syringe.

"Are you high?" I asked, incredulously. He said he had

forgotten that we were starting the shots that night (the shot that he was supposed to stick into my upper buttock in a smooth, dartlike motion), and he might have had a few bites of ice cream.

Pot ice cream. With his prescription from the OB/GYN, Ian could go to the Farmacy (yes, spelled like "farm") and get pot in various forms (pot butter, a lollipot, buzznana bread), because apparently good old-fashioned marijuana was no longer good enough. It was just old-fashioned. Pot was much stronger now, and came in various colors and blooms, like fancy teas, and it could be vaporized, used as a cooking aid, or made into a sundae.

I gave myself the shot that night, which was no small feat, and the next morning I tried to appeal to Ian on a scientific level. "There is evidence showing that pot affects sperm count, or sperm motility, which could be why we're having problems conceiving," I said. What I did not say was that if Ian was any indication, his stoned sperm were not likely to get off the couch, let alone make a baby.

On our next visit to the fertility clinic, an apparently unconvinced Ian asked our doctor if smoking pot once in a while might indeed be affecting his sperm count. And the doctor said no.

This was a male doctor.

I'm not saying that his gender had anything to do with the veracity of his answer, but it might have had something to do with the fact that he seemed amused rather than offended by Ian's "I told you so" jig that followed.

The doctor explained that their process involved spinning down the good (sober) sperm, and apparently there were enough of those guys that Ian's occasional habit would not hinder our ability to have a baby.

I was starting to hate doctors. And husbands.

Why wasn't it enough that I would have liked my husband to stop, that it would have meant something to me if he gave up pot, because I had given up alcohol, red meat, sugar, sushi, soft cheese, skinny jeans, my fear of injections, and three years of my life trying to have this baby? Why couldn't he give up marijuana?!

He didn't understand why I cared so much. I tried to explain again that he wasn't really present when he was high.

"Exactly," he agreed. "That's what I like about it."

He reminded me that he didn't watch sports, which is how most married men escaped. He didn't go to strip bars. He didn't drink much. He didn't play golf. So once in a while, he smoked pot. "What's the big deal? You do things *I* don't like," he pointed out.

Wait, what?

We were now on very thin ice because, once again, I was about to ask a question that I might not want to know the answer to, but I forged ahead. I asked him to name anything he didn't like about me, because, unlike him, *I* would be willing to change to make him happy.

He replied that he would never ask me to give up anything. Especially something I enjoyed.

Smart answer. This is why you should never marry a lawyer.

My rebuttal: "You wouldn't ask, because there's nothing I do that bothers you in the same way."

He considered for a minute and then muttered, no, there was something. I braced myself. Snacking? Snoring?

"Reality TV," he said a little triumphantly.

I felt that was completely different. In fact, it wasn't until I found myself up late at night a few days later watching *Little Chocolatiers* (a TLC show about two little people who are married and run a chocolate shop) that I realized Ian might be right—reality TV might be my drug of choice.

But just as there are various forms of pot, there are various forms of reality TV, I now explained to him, and some shows are good for you. Some inspire you to dream big and master a trade, like *Project Runway, Top Chef*, and HBO's *Cathouse*. Surely Ian didn't want me to stop watching *Cathouse*, the show about the gals at the Moonlite Bunny Ranch brothel in Nevada. That was benefiting both of us.

And some programs, I went on, make you feel good by showing you the power of transformation, like *The Biggest Loser* (which, I did not mention, I sometimes watched while eating dinner) and *What Not to Wear* (the British version, because the British stylists don't publicly flog you when they find t-shirts and leggings in your wardrobe).

Some shows, I had to admit, were empty calories, but I still ate them up. These included *The Bachelor, America's Next Top*

Model, *The Real Housewives of Atlanta/DC/Beverly Hills*, the reunion specials of *The Real Housewives of New Jersey*, and any season except the first of *Jersey Shore*. (That first season was not empty calories, it was a cultural crash course on guidos and guidettes, and I remain its staunch defender.)

And some shows you had to watch because everyone else was watching them, like *The Amazing Race*, *Survivor*, *The Voice*, *American Idol*, and *Dancing with the Stars*. I didn't watch all of these shows all of the time, I pointed out, and I certainly didn't bother watching the results shows.

Ian was concerned that I even knew the term "results show."

I told him I could see how some shows, when combined with other shows, might be too much of a good thing; for example: *Hoarders* and *Intervention*, *Ultimate Cake Off* and *Cake Boss*, *Dance Moms* and *Toddlers & Tiaras*, *Wife Swap* and *Supernanny*, *Little Chocolatiers* and anything. . . .

In fact, based on this list, it *could* be argued that I was watching an inordinate amount of reality television. And Ian did argue exactly that. He said I was watching so much *Intervention* that I might need an intervention. But that show, I insisted, was full of valuable cautionary tales for parents-to-be.

For example, from *Intervention* I learned that if you didn't ever tell your kid you loved him, he would turn to meth. He might not know that's *why* he was turning to meth, but if you only had said "I love you" a few times when he was growing up, he might not now be shooting up in your basement. And if he was shooting up in your basement, you had to kick him out. Stop bringing him soup. Stop loaning him money. Stop driving him to his dealer because you'd be less worried that way. You had to help him hit rock bottom, and then when he did, you and the rest of the family (including overweight cousins and the ex-girlfriend who met him when he was homeless and still somehow ended up being disappointed in him) had to read him a letter itemizing how he had hurt you, and why he needed to get help, and then, when he tried to leave the room shouting, "This is bullshit!"—*that's* when you told him you loved him! And because he had never heard those words from you, he would crumble into your arms and go to rehab and get his life together.

"Thus," I fumphered, "we should say 'I love you' often to our child. But if we don't, we can use it later for leverage."

Ian had by now convinced himself that my habit was in fact more harmful than his. So I brought out the big guns—*Extreme Makeover: Home Edition*—a guaranteed cry every time they "Move that bus!!!"

I love *Extreme Makeover: Home Edition*. Especially how the family members cover their eyes and scream when they first see their house, and again when they see the inside, and again in every room. All of the families, regardless of race or circumstance, cover their eyes and sometimes drop to their knees when the house is revealed. I think it's part amazement, part relief. This worry that they've been carrying around—how to provide for their children—has been lifted, and they can finally release all of the emotions they'd been holding back because they were trying to keep their family intact.

Maybe that's what I liked about the show, I patiently explained to Ian—the idea that a worry could be lifted. Although I still did worry for the families on the show. I worried what would happen to that youngest boy, the lover of science, when he grew up and brought a girl home to his room. How would he explain the giant microscope he's been sleeping under for ten years that the *Extreme Makeover* team custom designed for him? Or the dinosaur bed his teenage foster brother was still sleeping in across the hall? Did *Extreme Makeover* do *Extreme Home Redecorating*?

Ian wasn't sure what point I was making anymore, and frankly, neither was I, so I punted: "Honey, there are sick children living with mold, a girl who can't be exposed to sunlight needing special windows so she can move from room to room, children who have only torsos who need an elevator so they don't have to elbow their way up the stairs. And then there's you, a perfectly healthy man living in a beautiful home who 'needs' a man cave, and to get into that man cave he wants a bookshelf to slide open when you remove a certain book."

Ian conceded the bookcase was optional. What wasn't optional, apparently, was the fact that we both needed an escape from each other from time to time. All married people do. All of America does, measured by the popularity of reality shows. And if I was any indication of the state of the union (marital and national), viewership is up when you're down.

Regardless of whose avoidance strategy was healthier (mine), we could see that either, taken to excess, had the potential to hurt us more than heal us. So in the spirit of limiting our avoidance of each other, we both cut back. And Ian agreed to occasionally watch reality shows with me (and not make fun of them) when he was high, and I agreed to occasionally watch action movies with him in the Escape Pod when he wasn't.

It's not a perfect solution. I still wish Ian would give up pot completely, and he still wishes I didn't wish that, but that's the reality of marriage.

And despite these occasional rifts, I know I would not want to be married to anyone else, not even for a week.

I know this because I watch *Wife Swap*.

Our Romance Is Going to the Dogs

I remember crying in the shower. It was our first real impasse as a married couple, and I could not imagine how it could end without one of us having to move out. I hoped it would be the St. Bernard.

I will explain in a moment how, in our first year of marriage, Ian talked me into getting not only a dog, but a St. Bernard. As soon as we got home with this panting, slobbering beast, I knew we'd made a terrible mistake. I was hopeful that Ian might come to the same conclusion, but that didn't seem likely given that he was on the floor rolling around with a giant fur ball that may or may not have contained our dog. (Did I mention the shedding? There was a *lot* of shedding.)

Despite the dog's flaws—which were not so much "flaws" as "traits," Ian explained patiently, which worsened when the dog was nervous, and he told me I was making her nervous (*I* was making *her* nervous?)—despite her *traits*, Ian was already madly in love with Tinkerbell.

Yes, he liked the idea of naming her Tinkerbell, aka Tink, because she was so tiny. Ha ha ha help.

I couldn't say I hadn't seen this coming. Well, I hadn't seen a St. Bernard coming, exactly, which is ironic because you can see a St. Bernard coming from quite a distance. It's not like a Chihuahua, which you might miss and almost step on because it arrived in a purse. I'll say this for St. Bernards: they never arrive in a purse.

But I knew some kind of dog was inevitable, because when Ian and I had just started dating in New York, he talked a lot about wanting a dog. And I encouraged him, because I liked the idea of a boyfriend with a dog. It says good things about a guy if he can love and take care of a pet. I imagined Sunday brunches at outdoor cafés, Ian's scrappy little dog at my feet, having given me the full canine seal of approval, which would make Ian love me even more.

But Ian didn't feel it was fair to keep a dog in his tiny East Village apartment when he was working such long hours. Yes, the same apartment where I lived with him for two months was deemed unfit for a dog.

When we finally started looking for a larger New York apartment to rent together, I was so giddy that we were officially a "we" I didn't balk when Ian told our real estate agent that we needed a building that allowed pets. She felt that would limit our choices considerably and asked what kind of pet we had. That's when "we" went back to being "him" and "me," because I wanted to see as many apartments as possible. We were starting a life together; we might want a doorman, a view of the river, a loft. . . .

I was distracted visualizing the SoHo Us versus the West Village Us when I realized Ian was telling our real estate agent which breeds he liked, and how much our *imaginary* dog might weigh, because some buildings have weight limits. She smiled, which was not easy for a woman who had undergone so much plastic surgery, and asked if "pet-friendly" was a deal breaker. I said, "Not really," and Ian said, "Yes." That's when I realized this dog issue might come back to bite me in the ass.

I can feel the dog lovers among you starting to hate me, but I am not the villain in this story. I grew up with dogs. It just didn't seem like the time to get a dog when we were officially moving in together for the first time and had plans to travel. And then we got married and moved to my place in Los Angeles, and Ian wanted to have a baby right away, so again, it seemed the responsible thing to do was to have the baby, then get the dog.

Ian was frustrated by the dog delays, but he agreed to wait six more months and see how things looked on the baby front.

At six months exactly (Ian must have marked his calendar), we didn't appear to be getting a baby anytime soon, but apparently we were now scheduled to be getting a dog within the next few days. Ian would wake me every morning with candidates from dog rescue Web sites. When I suggested we talk about it more, he suggested we take it up in therapy.

This was especially annoying because couples therapy had been my idea. I thought it would help us iron out a few differences before we got married, like our feeling about houseguests. Ian wanted the same open-door policy he'd always had with friends and family, and I wanted the privacy and boundaries I'd established as someone who worked mostly from home.

The truth is I still thought of Ian as a houseguest. I was still surprised to see him every night and, even more so, every morning. It was a nice surprise, but it took some getting used to. So I felt that, under the circumstances, I was being extremely open to having guests in my home.

Of course, I felt lucky to be with a guy who was willing to go to therapy and confident enough to use my own therapist, since most men think your therapist will automatically take your side. I knew my therapist was a very wise, very fair person who probably *would* take my side in this case, because she knew how challenging it was for me to look out for my own interests. If I was this concerned about a dog, surely she would agree that Ian should defer to my wishes.

But the bitch agreed with Ian.

She agreed with him after all the years I'd spent in her office, all of the boyfriends who had been on her couch. (Seriously, almost everyone I ever dated had been to therapy with me, usually right around the time that I knew we should break up. Ian was the only man in my life with whom therapy had led to a stronger beginning rather than a quicker ending.)

My therapist reminded me that I had promised Ian six

months, and those six months were now up. She asked what I was worried about.

I admitted that I didn't like the idea of having to walk and feed the dog just because I was the one working at home. Ian said he would do all of that or get a dog walker to help. For how long? Forever. It would be his dog, and I could just enjoy it without any responsibility whatsoever.

I told her I was afraid it would be the end of romance. Ian said the dog would never be on the bed, and it would not mean less love for me; it would mean more love for all of us.

I said I worried the dog would be needy. Ian said that's why he wanted to get a big dog, because big dogs are less needy.

I was out of objections, and we were out of time. It had been fifty minutes and three years.

We were getting a dog. A big dog.

Just as there are Big and Tall shops for men, there's a place to get big and tall dogs. It's called Gentle Giants Rescue and Adoption, and I think I was in denial when Ian drove me there because I couldn't tell you where it was, only that it took us about two hours to find it. It is run by Burt Ward (*the* Burt Ward who was Robin on the TV series *Batman*, Ian enthused), and when we arrived we were "greeted by the herd." This is a tradition at Gentle Giants, because Burt wants you to get comfortable with the idea of large dogs, so he seats you on a bench and releases a herd of dogs that bound toward you as if you are dinner, and then, if you haven't blacked out, you notice tails wagging and heads lowering so you can pet them, and eventually the herd wins you over, although I think it's part charm, part intimidation.

Then the interminable audition process begins, and we were not the only people adopting a gentle giant that day. We agreed to let the folks with kids and dogs go first (your old dog is required to meet your new dog) before we realized that the canine candidates had to be brought out one at a time for health reasons. I'm not sure if it was for their health or ours, but Burt Ward's wife even changed her t-shirt every time she brought out a new puppy.

The puppies were deceiving, because all puppies are small. Buying a puppy at Gentle Giants seemed to me like buying a dinosaur egg, so I was relieved when Ian explained, when it was finally our turn, that we wanted a dog who was one or two years old so that we could bypass the puppy stage. He thought a puppy might be too much work, since we were trying to have a baby.

I began to think Ian might actually be capable of making this decision for us in a loving and logical way, and I'm embarrassed to admit that possibility hadn't occurred to me before. It also hadn't occurred to me that I might be the villain in this story. That's the problem with getting married: it's like looking into a mirror twenty-four hours a day. Your spouse reveals all of your flaws—not by pointing them out explicitly; just by being there. I have never enjoyed looking in a mirror. I always focus on what I don't like more than what I do. And now I was living with a mirror. And in that mirror I saw a control freak who didn't want to let her husband get a dog.

To be fair, Gentle Giants had great dogs—Great Danes, Great Pyrenees—and in that company a malnourished eighteen-month-old St. Bernard can look downright petite. And she was a "small" St. Bernard. I saw this as one of her most redeeming qualities, but I gather if you're in the market for a St. Bernard, she looks like the runt of the litter. It wasn't until we got her home that I realized we had the biggest dog in the neighborhood. And by neighborhood I mean the 467 square miles that comprise Los Angeles.

When she put her paws up on our outdoor balcony (as she loyally would when Ian would leave each morning), she looked like a person in a dog suit. And judging by the amount of hair I would vacuum up each day, it's amazing she still had the dog suit. Maybe the drool kept everything in place.

There was one not-so-terrible side effect of having a dog in the house. It now seemed, to me, that Ian and I belonged in the space and Tink did not. This was *our* space, *our* sanctuary. The dog had become the houseguest I hadn't been prepared for, which meant Ian had moved up in rank to permanent resident. It was me and Ian against the world.

But Ian didn't see it that way. He saw it as him and Tink against the world. Tink, being a rescue, had been in several homes already. Not everyone was game for taking care of a St. Bernard, especially a St. Bernard who was going to rack up some large veterinary bills before she was completely healthy.

In any case, Ian refused to give her up. He refused to be another human who disappointed her. It was an admirable quality in Ian, and it was also why I took to crying in the shower, where Ian couldn't see me. Except it's a glass shower, so he did see me (the mirror sees all!) and he joined me, and held me, and looked at me with equally sad eyes. He knew what I knew—there was no good solution to this problem. Then Tink padded in, and she didn't join us in the shower, but she had the same sad, swollen-eyed look.

It was not until later that I realized that it was not a look; it was a trait.

But at that moment, in the bathroom, I knew I had to make it work. And once I made peace with the fact that Tink was not just a houseguest, she stopped drooling and shedding and panting. I guess I was making her nervous. She sensed she was on the bubble.

I hesitate to admit that it was me who finally invited her up on the bed.

During her first six months she had gradually made her way at bedtime from downstairs, to the hallway outside of our bedroom, to the floor of our bedroom. When I beckoned her up to join us on the bed, she leapt so quickly it was as if she'd been waiting for the invitation her whole life. In one swift move, she jumped six feet into the air and landed directly between us.

And the longer our baby quest took, the more I grew to love and appreciate Tink. I can't imagine waiting so many years for a baby and not having Tink to hold on to, her big head on my shoulder (which, incidentally, is what I feared would happen once she was allowed on the bed, but I always imagined her on Ian's shoulder, not mine).

Now it was the three of us in the house—*our* house—and, as Tink seemed to think of it, *our* bed. Someday a baby might sleep between us, but for the moment, we held a small St. Bernard.

A Fine Mess

In any marriage, even the best marriage, there will come a day when you will wonder why you married this person.

At your wedding it's hard to fathom such a thing ever happening. This handsome, tuxedoed man is publicly binding his life to yours, looking into your eyes, and declaring his eternal devotion, and you think, *Never! It would have to snow inside my house before I would ever feel anything but love and gratitude for this man!*

Well, it snowed inside my house.

I am not saying that metaphorically. I am telling you it literally snowed inside my house, because one year, to kick off the holiday season, Ian had somehow decided—even though we still didn't have kids, even though I never said I missed snow—that I would enjoy a snow machine.

I don't know where to even begin or end this story.

Let's just start by saying that this wasn't *flakey* snow, not that I would have enjoyed flakey snow, but Ian did admit later he thought it would be flakey. This is the problem with ordering things like a snow machine online. You can never be sure if the snow will be just mildly annoying or marriage-ending annoying.

Instead the snow was *sudsy*. Sudsy like a washing machine was overflowing and spewing suds off my second-floor balcony and into my living room, where I was flipping through a magazine in front of the fire, having been instructed not to peek while Ian set up the Big Surprise.

Perhaps, in retrospect, the fact that Ian was playing "Let It Snow" on the stereo should have tipped me off, but I thought he was just setting a festive mood, and frankly, who would have guessed that any sane person (let alone a spouse who supposedly knew and loved me) would let it snow, let it snow, let it snow inside my house?

Maybe you've noticed that I am back to calling it *my* house, *my* second-floor balcony, *my* living room. Of course it was *our* house . . . unless you unleashed a snow machine inside of it, and then it reverted back to *my* house, the house I bought myself before I met you, the house I decorated, the house that contains *my* favorite leather chair that suddenly has a wet stain where *your* sudsy snow has just landed.

I have to admit, I had a bad feeling about the Big Surprise. It came in a big box, and there wasn't much I could think of that any woman would want that comes in a big box. Chocolate and jewelry come in small boxes. Clothes come in relatively small boxes. They say good things come in small packages; I say bad things come in big boxes.

Thus I was well prepared for something I might have to

fake being excited about. And I am on the fence about whether it is gracious or self-sabotaging to fake excitement over a gift that you don't love from your spouse. On the one hand, you want to reward his efforts and encourage future gift giving. On the other hand, that's the kind of flawed, codependent thinking that leads women to fake orgasms with men who still have no idea where the clitoris is. And those men have no idea they have no idea. That is the danger of faking.

So I was sitting there, debating whether to fake excitement about the new drum set for Rock Band or whatever it was that Ian got me that we couldn't really afford and didn't really need, when, as it happened, I didn't have time to fake a response. I had a genuine response in a voice I barely recognized, because, just as you don't know what your scream sounds like until you're actually screaming, you don't know what your *Mommie Dearest* voice sounds like until you/she/it shrieks: "*What the hell is happening?!*"

Now, let me tell you what the hell was happening. From above me large blobs of "snow" were falling and accumulating on the floor while also landing in clumps on the area rug, the coffee table, and (as I mentioned) my favorite leather chair. One clump stuck to the wall, which is not something snow does, by the way. Real snow does not land on a vertical surface and stick there, but this sudsy snow did stick until it slowly started to slide down, leaving a thin, wet trail in its wake, like a snail. I think it was this thin, wet trail—combined with the wet stain on the leather chair—that caused me to stand and yell, "*Stop, stop, stop, turn it off!*"

Amazingly, that was the first moment Ian realized the expression on my face was not joy but horror.

He turned the machine off and explained that the snow was nonstaining and nontoxic and could simply be "vacuumed up," which would have been nice to know before it began showering down on our sofa, but I guess that would have ruined the Big Surprise. Speaking of which, I was beginning to think the Big Surprise was that the man I married had no clue about me whatsoever.

Surely he'd noticed I was a neat freak. My parents had noticed, because I wasn't always a neat freak, but just as my tolerance for alcohol had weakened since college, so had my tolerance for messes. And that does make me feel like a freak. I don't like a house that looks too perfect. Actually, I do, but I don't like being the kind of person who needs her house to look perfect. In fact, once, back in my single days, when I had a date coming over, I intentionally put some dishes and a glass in the sink to avoid that perception. Some women fake orgasms; I faked a mess.

I know I have a little Rain Man in me: *That's not where that pillow goes, definitely, definitely* not *where it goes.* But when you're single and living alone, if you like things just so, you can have them just so. And when you come home at night, unless you've been robbed, things will still be just so. And then you get married, and nothing is ever just so again.

Mess tolerance was something I had been struggling with even before the snow machine incident. It's a topic all couples face at some point. All straight couples, at least. I can't help but notice that most of my gay male friends, whether single or cohabitating, have gorgeous Zen homes that look and smell like boutique hotels. I dream of their clutter-free counters and perfectly organized closets. I think cleaning should be called "gaying things up" instead of "straightening things up."

Still, I was happy, when I married Ian, to finally have a straight spouse in the house.

The same could not be said of my housekeeper.

My housekeeper came with my house when I bought it in 1997. The people who lived there before me kept things much neater, she managed to communicate, despite her sometimes spotty English. At first I was offended, but once I got used to enjoying an immaculate home every Tuesday, I found it easier to maintain Wednesday through Monday, and eventually we settled into a rhythm of mutual appreciation and respect, except for one square-shaped antique Chinese wooden rice bucket, which I always liked at an angle in the corner and she liked pushed directly into the corner.

We agreed to disagree (aka I put it back at an angle every Tuesday night), but I didn't mind, because given that I was learning to keep things pretty clean myself, that rice bucket was the only sure sign my housekeeper had been there. In fact, sometimes it was unclear who was keeping the house clean for whom.

But while it was just the two of us (me and her), if something was out of place or missing, we noticed. That's why it should not have surprised me one day, almost a decade ago, when she asked: "What happened to Steve?"

Steve had been my boyfriend of three years, and when we broke up, I forgot to tell my housekeeper. Actually, I didn't forget: it had never entered my mind that I needed to. But there she was, folding laundry, asking me about Steve. And he'd been out of my life for months, so clearly she was waiting to ask, waiting to see if he was just busy, or out of town. And in that moment I realized that either she is secretly glad she no longer has to do Steve's laundry on occasion, or she is worried I might die alone. And those two things might not be mutually exclusive.

I think it was the latter, because she proceeded to tell me, even though I hadn't asked, that she had been married to her own husband for thirty-two years. "Thirty-two years," she repeated.

That conversation haunts me still. I had had no idea that anyone—other than my parents—had been concerned. So I thought she would be relieved when I finally came home to Los Angeles with Ian. But she wasn't relieved once she saw how Ian lived, which is to say he left evidence of life around the house.

She was used to dealing with much less life. She had taken care of my house for a long stretch when nobody lived there, while I was working on *Sex and the City* in New York. Sure, she had to deal with me when I was home between seasons, but by then, I liked the house the way she liked the house, so it was a wash, literally.

But then I brought Ian into the house, and Ian brought Tink into the house, and Tink brought sand into the house—something I had managed to avoid in ten years of living at the beach. So believe it or not, I had been feeling badly *for my housekeeper* until this particular evening I'm describing when a snow machine had appeared in the house.

It was a Tuesday evening, so the housekeeper had just left. Let me repeat: *Our housekeeper had just left.* This was the one day a week when the house was spotless, when everything was returned to order, when she would work her magic and drive away. Certainly Ian knew *that* about me, how much I loved cleaning day.

Maybe he thought the house would be superclean after this veritable indoor car wash, but instead it looked as if a rave was happening in our living room. And I said as much. In fact, I probably said more.

And that was the moment I realized the expression on Ian's face was not remorse but disappointment. And he was not disappointed in the snow machine, as I felt he should be as a consumer. He was disappointed in *me*.

He had had ideas about how this night would go, and never mind that he had snowed on my living room; I had rained on his parade.

He had imagined us dancing in the snow. (He was still looking down at me from the balcony when he confessed this, so we were kind of a reverse Romeo and Juliet, in more ways than one.)

And Ian does not abandon a plan easily, so he smiled and said, "C'mon, one dance." And then he turned on the snow again and hurried downstairs to join me, still hopeful the evening could be salvaged, possibly even made romantic.

And I thought, *What if this is one of those moments, like the night we officially moved in together in New York?* Ian had wanted to eat Chinese food while sitting on boxes, and I had wanted to unpack the boxes and get our lives in order. And he finally said he was going to a bar if I was not going to be "fun," and I worried he would go to a bar anytime I wasn't fun, and furthermore, I might not always be fun, and what then? Of course, the next morning, I regretted everything. Why had I been so concerned with unpacking that I couldn't enjoy our first night in our first joint apartment? That's a once-in-a-lifetime thing! It still makes me sad thinking about it. So that morning, our first Monday morning waking up together in our new place, I said I thought we should have a certain number of do-over days in our relationship. We should each get, say, three days that didn't count against you, no matter what you did. And Ian said, "Great, see you on Thursday."

Okay, that was funny. But the truth is you don't get do-overs. Certain moments in life never come back.

And it occurred to me now, with the snow falling wetly around me, that maybe this was one of those moments I might forever regret not enjoying. So I tried. And it was one of the hardest things I've ever done, but I am telling you honestly, I tried to smile and dance with Ian in the snow.

Until two seconds later, when my shoes started to slip and slide in the suds, and I was getting faux snow in my hair, and I yelped, "*I can't do it!*" And I ran outside and buried my head in my hands, and although to the casual observer it might seem that, once again, I was the not-fun one, all I could think was, *Why the hell did I marry this person?*

And I imagined that Ian was standing inside, in the snow, thinking the same thing.

And it wasn't like in the movies. We never looked at each other and started laughing hysterically. The whole night was kind of terrible, especially during the cleanup process (which was, in fact, a process).

First of all, I was surprised that I was expected to help, but I decided to pick my battles. I did not, for example, point out that the bubbles did not simply "vacuum up." The vacuum mostly just pushed the bubbles around.

To be honest, I still don't fully understand what the bubbles were made of, because they did not lose mass or melt, even once vacuumed. In fact, we used a see-through vacuum (we actually used *all* of our vacuums, and a few mops), and once it was clearly full of bubbles, that was it—there was no more room. Does that seem like standard bubble behavior to you? I'm pretty sure NASA has something to do with these bubbles.

Then Ian and I got into another disagreement about whether something could be designated for "indoor use only." This happened because I suggested that perhaps snow *outside* of our house might have been the way to go. I could have come home to the one house in Los Angeles surrounded by a lovely blanket of snow. Or he could have put the snow machine on our roof, and we could have been sitting by the fire, and he could have pointed out, "Look! It's snowing outside!" *That* might have been romantic.

"It's for indoor use only," he maintained. And I maintained, "Nothing is for indoor use only. If you can use it indoors, you can use it outdoors, unless it's so poisonous it would kill animals outdoors, and then it shouldn't be indoors either." We went round and round with this, and we still haven't resolved it. I did have to admit that the stains on the chair and wall did miraculously disappear, to which Ian replied dryly, "It wasn't miraculous. It's nontoxic and non-staining."

Finally, as if readying it for burial, Ian placed the snow machine back into the big box between two plastic containers of bubble refills, which, to my surprise, he pulled out from under the bathroom sink where he had already stashed them for, I guess, the *next time* we wanted snow in the house? And then he said he would give the snow machine to someone at work "who would appreciate it."

I had to bite my tongue to avoid further insulting of the snow machine, not to mention the person "who would appreciate it." (Who might that be? Someone who hated her house? Someone who was having one of those parties where everyone paints graffiti on the walls because he was moving— *that* kind of person?)

As we carried several Hefty bags of bubbles outside and put them into the trash, Ian reminded me that sometimes I loved his grand gestures. I couldn't remember one that I loved until he said, "When I proposed, on the beach, on a horse?"

I admitted that that had been a good one (maybe because the horse hadn't been in our living room?), but that's the thing about romantics—you can't romanticize them. They can be hit or miss.

As it turned out, there was a lovely woman in Ian's office who had two toddlers and a linoleum kitchen, and apparently she made snow in the kitchen, and her husband loved it and laughed, and the kids loved it and laughed and played, and they all had so much fun they invited more kids to come back and enjoy more snow on Christmas Day.

So maybe the gift had just been too early—several years and one linoleum kitchen too early. And it was not lost on me that this gift ended a year during which Ian and I had gotten further from, not closer to, having kids of our own (more about that in a moment). But this was also a year (other than when it snowed inside my house) during which Ian and I had gotten closer to, not further from, each other.

We did not get closer with the housekeeper, though. She never learned about the snow machine—I made sure of that for Ian's sake, fearful it might put her over the edge and lead to some kind of homicide/suicide by toxic cleaning products. But as her workload got heavier, so did her sighs, and eventually, her sighs were all I could hear.

I knew she was upset about the dishes in the sink, Ian's clothes on the floor, the unmade bed, the bathroom sink sprawl . . . because so was I.

But Ian was trying. He was making an effort—the dishes in the sink were unstaged now, but Ian used the kitchen nightly, so . . . dishes happen. The clothes on the floor had dwindled down to only that day's clothes. The unmade bed was better than Ian's attempt to make the bed, which had the effect of a badly wrapped present: sometimes, it's better not to bother. Ian even agreed to get Tink groomed every other week to cut down on the dog hair.

We were all trying to adjust to life together, so why was it feeling most trying to our housekeeper? She was supposed to make it better, to put things back in order, at least once a week. Her frustration and intolerance only highlighted my own.

So I had to end the relationship. Not with Ian. With her. And she had been my longest relationship ever.

I really tried to make it work. I gave her space (I basically invented reasons to leave the house when she was cleaning), and several raises (even though my friends were paying less for their nannies), but nothing seemed to make her happy. We both knew it would never be like it had been, and the baby Ian and I had been waiting for all these years (apparently she'd been waiting, too, quietly, just like she'd been waiting for Steve to come back) would not make things better, mess-wise.

So we said our good-byes, and she tearfully gave me back my key despite my insistence that I had other copies, please, let's not make this worse. . . .

Then I hired a new housekeeper who didn't know the house any other way.

I, too, need to let go of remembering the house as it had been. There's life in it now, and we were hoping to add more life still.

But every so often, when Ian leaves town, I wander from room to room and tidy up, and organize, and put everything just so. And then I wake up the next morning in my big house, which now seems big for one person, too big really. And it slowly dawns on me: everything will be exactly as I left it.

I cannot explain how thrilling that is. Unless you're gay. Or my ex-housekeeper.

Eggspecting

I was finally pregnant, thanks to a twenty-three-year-old restaurant hostess in New York City.

No, she did not seat me next to a swarthy Italian stranger who impregnated me.

She was our egg donor.

Most of the time I was able to forget that we had had to use an egg donor. I felt as if the baby growing inside of me was thoroughly mine. I had the same joys and fears and nausea as every other pregnant woman in the world, except when I was annoyed with Ian, and then it was as if I'd been forced to carry a love child he had conceived with some random twenty-three-year-old.

Only she hadn't been random. We'd sifted through over 300 profiles to find her. Ian said it was the first time since getting married that he could look at girls online without afterward having to press "delete history." I try not to dwell on that comment.

So how did I become my own surrogate? How does any

woman find herself asking: "Can I borrow an egg? I'm trying to make a child."

For us, after three and a half years of trying to get pregnant on our own ("on our own" being a euphemism for the army of experts we were paying to help us get pregnant), we finally discovered the medical explanation for our fertility problems.

I was old.

No doctor actually said that, but at forty-three, I finally realized the gentle suggestions we were getting from friends and experts about "other options" like adoption and an egg donor were not "other options." They were our only options.

Of course, women *can* get pregnant at forty-three. You hear stories about it all of the time (when you're forty-three), and those stories become a ray of hope and also the bane of your existence, because they keep you from moving on to Plan B.

The thing about Plan B is that it's comforting to have . . . when you're still on Plan A. But when the thick, cushy rug of Plan A gets yanked out from under you (even if that rug involved endless IVF treatments and shots in the ass), Plan B can require a period of adjustment.

But we didn't have time to adjust. We'd already spent three and a half years in the effort. And every new road to getting a baby seemed like a long and winding one, so we decided to just get on some road, any road, and adjust on the way.

In that spirit we headed to Orange County for an all-day adoption seminar. It was sponsored by an organization called

Resolve, and our lack of resolve became clear when the first three speakers broke into tears, and we just wanted to break for lunch.

The problem wasn't what they were saying about adoption; it was *how* they were saying it. I have a rule that a person who is speaking publicly should not be more emotional than the people in the audience. I devised that rule when Ian and I heard a woman perform a story about how she had to bake a wedding cake for two lesbian friends who were getting married while her cat was sick, and the story just got more and more painful until it ended with "And then my cat died." And she was in tears, and nobody else was. I turned to Ian and said, "Not a dry eye on the stage."

So, she's my cautionary tale. Because of her—and her dead cat—I always try to make sure that I am not the only one moved by whatever story I happen to be telling.

But that was not the case at this adoption seminar. It seemed (to me, at least) that most of the people listening not only were not moved—they were not happy. I think most of them, like us, were still mourning the loss of Plan A, and the result was some displaced anger at the speakers and at one another, which explains why Ian almost came to blows with a guy who cut him off while he was asking a question.

Now, let me just say I have many friends who have adopted, and they all have beautiful, smart, funny, confident children. And these friends could not be happier or prouder as parents, which is why I always thought adoption would be our default Plan B.

What I had not realized was that Ian and I would not be able to reconcile our adopted baby. I wanted to adopt from China, and he wanted to adopt from Africa. At this seminar those were two completely different breakout sessions. And all future discussions on the subject left us both feeling depressed and vaguely racist.

So I finally asked Ian—who had originally joked that if I couldn't be part of the formula genetically there was no reason to pass on *his* messed-up genes, if he would want to consider an egg donor. And he lit up. Like a kid at Christmas. Which made it clear that, although he hadn't wanted to be the one to suggest it, part of him had been secretly hoping I would be willing to try an egg donor next.

Maybe a better wife would have offered that up right away. "I want to have *your* baby, honey. That's why I married you! Forget the egg; the most important thing is your sperm!" But that sounded too sexist to stomach. And it was my stomach that would be expanding, which, to me, always seemed like the *least* exciting part of the process.

But once we decided to go the egg donor route, I agreed to carry the baby, because . . . I don't know . . . it just seemed like I should be involved somehow.

We began with an egg donor seminar (you'd think we'd have learned our lesson, but at least this one was only a couple of hours long), where we felt as if we'd finally found our people, until one of our people asked if her fourteen-year-old daughter could be her egg donor. And the doctor leading the seminar had to politely tell her that there might be some is-sues with that, like that it was *sick*.

He didn't say that, but it was implied when he explained that, if her daughter was a virgin, the procedure might break her hymen.

Wow. I thought losing my virginity in a frat house was unromantic.

He also said that her daughter might agree to that plan to please her mother, but she might later regret being the *mother of her sister*. Based on that disturbing discussion, we decided our donor should be a complete stranger. And that we should stop going to seminars.

Ian then proceeded to do what any good husband would do: he tried to find an egg donor who looked and seemed the most like me.

And although that was a sweet sentiment, I said, "What the hell are you doing?! We need to go better, stronger, faster! We need someone with a good metabolism who is wildly ath-letic with long legs and shiny hair!"

I became a total boy about it. I was only interested in mod-els and athletes. I didn't care if they were smart. We could teach our kid everything he or she needed to know, but the gift of hotness, that's something you're born with. I found one donor who looked like Megan Fox, and I showed Ian her profile and he asked, somewhat baffled, "What do you like about her?"

I said, "Look at her!"

He thought she sounded cold in her essay answers, and she had typos, which was a deal breaker for him, despite my warning that he would have to explain to our future daughter that she could have been a knockout but we wanted her to be able to spell "autumn" instead.

Then Ian (who is not black, in case there is any confusion) decided maybe we should use an African American egg donor, forcing me once again to feel like the racist who just wanted a white kid.

I have nothing against black people! I just didn't see why, if we were going through the trouble of actually giving birth to a child, we needed to advertise to the world that it wasn't biologically my child. (Which, granted, would also have been the case with a kid who looked like Megan Fox.)

I know it's a small world, after all, but it's my uterus, after all, so does everyone need to know it wasn't my egg? Ian said it was more likely that people would think I had slept with a black man. That's a sexier version of events, but it was still not the impression I was looking forward to projecting as a family.

We finally enlisted the help of a friend of a friend who finds surrogates and donors for a living, and she had had twins herself using an egg donor, so she understood what we were going through. She had actually mingled her own eggs with those of her donor, so she still wasn't sure whether her boys are genetically her own or not. She planned to have a test done eventually, but for the time being, she liked the plausible deniability.

I thought about doing that, too, but what was the point? I knew my eggs. Their response would have been: "We're tired. You kids go ahead. Go have fun."

She put out an APB to all of her colleagues at ovum donor agencies (yes, in Los Angeles even eggs have agents), telling them we were a great couple and explained what we were looking for, and somehow our perfect donor showed up.

Ian and I both knew she was The One, which was a strangely bonding experience. We loved everything she had written. We loved her photos. We loved that she had studied abroad and played the oboe and was an artist and was planning to go to law school. It was only later, when it was time to do the embryo transfer, that I went online (to visit her profile?) and realized that she had graduated and was now working as a restaurant hostess in New York City.

I was worried. What had happened to law school? Ian said that she was probably saving money for tuition. In New York, restaurant hostesses make good money . . . because they're *hot*. So we were getting everything plus hotness, he reasoned.

That Ian—he knows just what to say to a girl who's about to get pregnant by another girl.

There were moments, leading up to this pregnancy, when I hadn't been sure why we'd been jumping through so many hoops to have a baby, and once I asked Ian to remind me why we were working so hard in what seemed like such an uphill battle. Maybe we weren't meant to have a kid. To which he replied, "We both live life fully. This is a big part of life. We're not missing it."

Vow Now

The jury is still out on whether it's the most beautiful or most embarrassing part of a wedding when a bride and groom read their own vows. It's certainly preferable to somebody else reading their vows, as was the case when my friend Marie was given the honor of reading a male friend's vows at his wedding. Even the bride would admit that that was just plain weird.

I've heard a groom ask his bride to vow to support the Pittsburgh Steelers.

I've seen a shy, normally stoic policeman whisper his vows when he got too emotional to continue aloud, and even though we couldn't hear what he was saying to his beloved, it brought most of the guests, me included, to tears.

It's too late for me, especially after including my vows in this book, to pretend I'm someone who would whisper them. In fact, I had so much to say on my Big Day that the wedding planner had to tell the caterer to hold dinner.

And, full disclosure, those were not the only vows I've written.

Ian and I write new vows each year on our anniversary.

Before you throw up, let me clarify that these annual vows are not all sunshine and roses. We do not quote songs or literature, or write our feelings in verse. Ian *can* speak in verse on any subject you give him, as I've mentioned, but that's more of a party trick, albeit a party trick that hooked me the first night I met him and the rest is history, a history that has been nicely chronicled, thanks to our yearly vows. These vows are a bit like a Christmas letter that we send only to each other, which is about as wide a distribution as most Christmas letters should get, but again, I'm not one to preach about discretion.

Our annual vows not only help us remember the past, they make "forever" seem much less daunting. How can anyone vow to love someone forever with a straight face? I mean, you do it because *not* to do it would definitely put a damper on the wedding, but Ian and I decided early on it was much more manageable to vow to love each other one year at a time. We don't automatically assume we're in it for the long haul. We hope we are, but every June on our anniversary, we end our vows by actively signing up for another year (which is wildly romantic until someone doesn't).

So far, neither of us has terminated our love lease, but some years it's harder to re-up than others. It's like a third, fourth, or fifth tour of duty in Iraq. You've *been* all you can be. You know what the enemy is capable of. Why volunteer for more?

That's an exaggeration, of course. Every year of our marriage has not been like a year of combat.

Only Year Five was. Year Five, we were lucky to get out alive.

Someone recently asked me if marriage was as hard as people say. I think life is harder than people say, and marriage ideally makes it easier to get through the hard times in life. That was the only good news about Year Five. It was not Husband versus Wife. It was us against the world, as I always thought it should be, except the world seemed to be winning.

I wrote my Year Five vows while I was still reeling, when I couldn't see the light at the end of the tunnel. That's the most helpful time to write, I think, because how you feel about your spouse during the lowest lows is just as important to acknowledge and remember as how you feel during the highs. Time has a way of putting things in perspective, of assigning meaning. But some years can't be wrapped up in a pretty little package. Some years are just hard.

When we got married, I wished we were younger, that we had five years to be just a couple. On our fifth anniversary, I felt as if the universe was laughing like a maniac and saying: "You got your five years! How do you vow *now*?"

This is how I vowed:

Year Five

I am re-upping for another year, let's just say that right now.

But we've been through so much in five years. Too much. And I only realized that in the last month, I guess, when everything broke down, and now I just want to watch *Top Chef* and sleep.

And yet by some standards, what have we been through, really? Nobody's dying.

And by other standards (ours), this thing we've wanted, a baby, has been so elusive, and even though I know it's not my fault, nothing intentional on my part, my role in not getting you this thing you've wanted so badly has been tough. I feel like I, and my body, have carried a lot of the responsibility for not carrying, or carrying and losing, two babies.

I want us to be happy.

I want us to be done trying.

I want us to be a family.

I want us to move forward through this period of waiting.

Uch, how to begin describing Year Five.

Year Four ended with such relief and joy and gratitude, and still for some reason the universe saw fit to pull the rug out one more time. In July 2009, after we finally cleared the first trimester hurdle, there was cramping and several visits to our doctor, and then two trips to the hospital in one day—one where we saw the baby move on an ultrasound and were temporarily relieved; a second that was the late-night D&C to ensure that all hope was, in fact, gone.

What I remember about that first visit to the hospital was wanting to be home, then the cramping getting worse at home and calling the doctor for painkillers, then you bringing me warm biscuits (and me worrying that biscuits, my favorite food, might get ruined forever along with everything else), then going into the bathroom and realizing what was happening and saying *Shit Shit Shit*. And then you coming in and dealing, somehow, I don't know how, calling the paramedics, Tink licking my hand as they carried me out of the house, and then the ride in the ambulance with the sun through the back window setting behind us over the beach.

Is it weird I remember the sunset being bittersweet and pink and kind of beautiful? I think there was some relief that what we were dreading would happen all week had happened, and we were no longer waiting for it to happen, but then there was the horrible sadness setting in that it had happened—that was the sunset I saw from the back of the ambulance.

I remember you calling my parents from the ambulance to tell them the news, and holding my hand. You were worried only about me. For so long, you wouldn't leave my side.

At the hospital you told me you ran into that annoying Irish nurse who had said some kind of prayer for us earlier that wasn't answered, probably because of her thick accent.

You cried to our doctor at 1 A.M. after the surgery. She was supposed to deliver our baby and instead she had to deliver the news that we had lost the baby because I had gone into early labor. Labor. That's why I carried our donor egg baby. That's what we wanted to experience. And now, this experience, I will never be able to share with girlfriends when they tell their war stories. I will think of it, but I won't say anything.

That first visit to the hospital—not the second—I brought a bag of all of the good luck charms our friends had given me, at my request, for my birthday two months earlier. Then, at home, a paramedic had to remove my four-leaf clover bracelet in order to insert the IV. He said, "Do you need this?" And I said, "I guess not. I don't think it's working anymore."

You were there. I was there. It is a place we revisit on our saddest, darkest days, so I don't need more details here except to remind you and myself that I never felt more taken care of. I joked later that you don't often get to crash test a relationship, but that felt like our crash test. And you passed. You were better than anyone could have expected you to be, better than I would have been. You were losing everything— again—and you cared only that I be okay. That is love. If I had to define love for myself, I would look to that moment and say I married exactly the right man and he is the best man I know.

That was in July, such a short time after those bright-eyed letters we wrote about Year Four. So then the healing. You took off work. We were never closer, physically or otherwise, because the pain was like glue. For a month or more we were hard to reach, but we were together in the grief.

We ran away to a dog-friendly hotel in Santa Barbara. We were both so drained we talked about pulling a Sophie's choice and taking too much Advil or whatever people take that isn't too awful, and just ending it, lying in each other's arms.

But Tink was in her usual place between us on the bed, and we knew we couldn't leave her behind. And we couldn't take her with us into that good night because then we would no longer be remembered as the tragic victims of infertility heartache; we would be the monsters who killed their dog.

We actually had that conversation, and because of Tink (and our families, and each other, but mostly because of Tink) we had to soldier on. Our rescue rescued us.

Although in the hospital we both agreed we were done trying to have our own baby, it took me three months to feel like pursuing anything else. You were very patient, and I know that was hard. I just wanted to wait until I could feel something other than sadness to kick off a new process. You said you wanted me to be excited. I wasn't sure I would ever feel excitement again.

I went to some film festivals with the short film I directed (including the Feel Good Film Festival, where I didn't feel so good). We tried to see friends and movies, but nothing made us feel better. You were eager to move on. I was still gun-shy.

We traveled every month, as if we could leave the grief behind.

In August we stayed at a famous hotel on the bluffs of Big Sur, and I had a panic attack in our hobbit hole of a room. It was built into a hillside. There was moss on the roof. It was the room I picked after years of looking longingly at their Web site, it was the room on their postcard, and I couldn't breathe.

In September you went on a surf trip to Mexico and tried to stay by losing your passport. Who could blame you? (Actually, it was stolen, and you worked very hard to get back over the border and home to me.) In October I went to New York and worked on a theater project with Liz and Elisa and Julie, and I'm not sure if it was New York, or the friends, or the theater, but I begin to feel like I had a pulse again.

As the holidays approached, we started researching adoption in earnest. I finally felt ready. I actually felt excited. We met with friends who had adopted and who were adopted. We started working with a domestic adoption lawyer and made a scrapbook for potential birth mothers, and got in all of our forms in record time, and the sight of you cradling the Resusci Baby during our infant CPR course reminded me how much you needed a real one.

You got me a snow machine. Again, you *really* need a child.

A television pilot I had written two years earlier came back to life. *Love Bites*. I turned our hotel room in Whistler into a production office while you were snowboarding and heliboarding, and you were fantastic, and we were both golden.

And that pilot process for me was so good, such a good experience; I felt so confident and happy and it seemed like the silver lining of not having a child yet—that I got to film that show, and that I was proud of it, and that I felt like I ran it so well.

And then when it made the NBC fall schedule in the plum time slot of 10 P.M. Thursday nights, I had a nervous breakdown.

Among other things, my virgin was pregnant.

The wonderfully talented, highly in demand actress we

got for the role of my main character, "The Last Virgin in Virginia," was pregnant.

I was one of the first people she told. She felt horrible about it, said she would understand if I wanted to do the show without her.

But I didn't want to do the show without her, and I didn't want a pregnancy (even if it wasn't mine) to be anything but joyful if I could help it.

I was in denial that it would change the show. I thought I could handle it. I thought wardrobe would handle it. There were so many moving pieces, and I was in charge of all of them.

Meanwhile, there was a birth mother (the third we had talked to), but this time, it seemed real. There would be a baby in a month, she said.

Again, I couldn't breathe. I was already having panic attacks at work. But a baby. Was this *our* baby?

You thought it was. You got attached. I liked the birth mother on the phone but had reservations about meeting her in L.A. Then she showed up unannounced, and you met her and liked her and I was dragging my feet, which was so frustrating to you, and then our lawyer said her story didn't check out; she was not for us.

And then you shut down. It was one more disappointment than you could take. This was all around our anniversary. You threw a beautiful dinner party with our very closest friends, and I felt naked. I still feel naked. I feel like all of the wounds of all of this pain and frustration and bad timing had come together such that I could not enjoy or even hold on to the idea of the birth of a baby or the birth of a show.

I just stepped down as show runner, the day after our anniversary.

And you are not used to seeing me this weak and scared, and I know it is scaring you.

Believe me, I hope to feel like myself again soon. Nobody misses me more than me.

So how to look forward to next year?

Because I do wish to sign up for another year, but I would like things to be different.

I would like to give myself and ourselves a fucking break.

I would like to get a break from the universe on this baby thing before we're collecting social security.

I would like to remember what my show was about. What was so funny about love? Sometimes love bites.

I wanted my show to be optimistic. I want to be optimistic again.

I didn't want it to be dark. I didn't want these vows to be dark, but I feel dark.

But you didn't mind that I stayed home today, on Independence Day, and watched a *Top Chef* marathon, and then we went up to the roof deck to watch the fireworks, and Tink jumped into the hammock with us, and we didn't tip over.

This was a hard year that began and ended with loss.

And I gave up something that doesn't come around often for a writer. I gave up my baby, in a sense, by giving up the reins of my show. I don't know how that was related to every-thing else we've been through, but I'm sure it was.

Maybe I'm clearing space, not just for a baby, but for our relationship. I think we need some TLC.

So, here I am, broken and dented, and I wish to sign up for another year, if you'll have me.

Love, your wife

Ian's Page

Let me just say (before anyone else does) that I know I am fortunate to have *any* partner, let alone a partner like Ian, in this baby quest. I have female friends who have gone through it alone, and I am in awe of their strength and resiliency.

But trying to produce a person with another person has its challenges. Not all couples survive. Every step and misstep along the way, you have to hope you're still on the same page.

Ian and I somehow remained on the same page until Year Five, and then things got so bad, he needed his own page.

Literally.

He decided to write about what we'd been through trying to have a baby.

I encouraged this at first, because I find journaling to be therapeutic and clarifying (even though I hate the word "journaling"—I don't know why it's not just called "writing"), but Ian's journaling seemed to be bringing him stress rather than comfort. For months he would mutter that he had to finish his "essay," which, I kept reminding him, did not need to be finished, did not need to be an essay; it was just for him.

But at some point, it wasn't just for him. It was for all men who had experienced similar losses, and when Ian finally shared it with me, I saw why he had needed to write it, and why he needed to finish it, and why men (and women) needed to read it.

So here it is—Ian's page—because this baby odyssey is our story, not mine. And because he was able to be more honest than I was about what we lost along the way.

A Father's Story: The Baby We Didn't Have

BY IAN WALLACH

It started perfectly. A rocking romance, magical wedding, decadent honeymoon, came home pregnant. My wife stomps out of the bathroom, half smiling, half accusatory, holding a plastic stick with a plus sign and yelling, "Ian, you got me pregnant!" Thirteen weeks later, we see the color flee from the face of our OB/GYN, and he tells us that this being was not meant to be.

"Specialist" was a title with which we would become too familiar. Specialist number one told us that we needed a D&C (dilation and curettage—in this case, a fancy term for ending a pregnancy). Over the next few years, more specialists explained more acronyms, like IUI (intrauterine insemination) and IVF (in vitro fertilization). We tried to understand the science behind each procedure, made ourselves believe we did, and gave each one a shot. Money rolled out while bad news washed in. And then several specialists (and one acupuncturist) suggested we try donor eggs.

A donor gave us eleven eggs and two chances. One procedure required many injections and five eggs but brought only frustration and sadness. After the second attempt, which used the remaining six eggs, we waited for the phone call. I promised I would take it, because my wife had answered all the others. It came late, which we decided wasn't good. But then something so unexpected happened: we did not get bad news.

Suddenly we were able to spend days, and then weeks, sharing a secret that seemed to cure an invisible injury. Weeks became months. We saw a moving head on a monitor. Later, tiny hands. We heard racing heartbeats (that I'd record on my iPhone). Three months in, we braced for the same fear-inducing test—the "nuchal fold," or neck measurement, scan—that had led to heartbreak once before. Somehow, still, there was no bad news.

A doctor—a specialist, even—said words like "healthy" and "female." On the short drive home, we quickly agreed on a name. We began designing the baby's room and thinking how our lives would change. We sent a global e-mail with the subject line "Congratulations to Us." I wrote, "Yesterday we passed the three-month-now-it's-okay-to-speak-about-it deadline, so we can announce that we are expecting a healthy baby girl to arrive in early January."

Two weeks later my wife woke me to say she was nervous and felt cramps. An ultrasound confirmed all was fine (and another, three days later, did as well). But three days after that, there was a lot of blood and a trip to the ER. Once again we were told that all was fine, shown images of the baby moving, and sent home.

My wife's cramps worsened. The doctor on call suggested Tylenol. When the pain sharpened, the doctor asked me to locate an open pharmacy to get Vicodin. My wife went to the bathroom, came back to bed, returned to the bathroom, and screamed. I knew.

I told her not to look down. (She had.) Still connected to her, facing west and not moving, was the physical embodiment of what we had only ever seen on-screen. Autopilot clicked on. I looked for a container, knowing I had to save everything. A colored pint glass was by the sink, and I washed it out. My wife moved to the rim of the bathtub. I collected what had fallen and ran to call 911.

I told the dispatcher that my wife had miscarried. He asked me to describe what happened and told me that she would probably be going into shock and I needed to cover her with blankets. I didn't want to go where I couldn't see her, and the blankets were more than thirty feet away, down the hall. I was stuck. The dispatcher told me to give the phone to my wife and go get the blankets. When I returned, she was crying less. The pain, which she hadn't known was labor, was subsiding.

In under five minutes the doorbell rang, and I ran

downstairs. Four paramedics rushed in, asking questions that somehow I was able to answer: "Where's your wife?" "Where is the fetus?" "Is it intact?" "How far along?" One of them scooped up our panicked dog and plopped her in another bathroom. These kind, brilliant men then flirted with my wife while simultaneously telling her that she was going into shock (explaining her jitterbug legs). They placed her on a chair and carried her down three flights of stairs. Leave it to my wife—at this moment—to joke about, and apologize for, her weight. Her beautiful, stunning, sexy, pregnancy weight.

Fire trucks and ambulances do little for discretion. The whole neighborhood was outside and knew what had happened. I reached the doctor on call and asked which hospital to go to. She seemed surprised and asked, "You called the paramedics?" I remember thinking, but not saying, *Yes, considering that my bloody wife is convulsing and our child's in a pint glass*. The kind man in the ambulance told us we were right to call for help, that 911 is there for situations that people can't handle on their own.

Our regular, more empathetic doctor drove from her home to meet us at the hospital and perform the surgery. Another D&C, necessary to make sure that what we knew was gone was completely so. Two hours later, my wife and I took a cab home.

In the morning, I retrieved the two-week-old celebratory e-mail, cut and pasted the names of the recipients, and informed everyone that the pregnancy had ended and we needed some private time. And then we witnessed different forms of the art of consolation.

The first wave was simply brilliant. Friends tiptoed up to our door, set down plates of macaroni and cheese, lasagna, sandwiches, or fruit, rang the bell—and left. How did I not know of this amazing practice? It was exactly what we needed: a combination of nourishment, respect, privacy, and love (unfortunately, a mere month later, we'd realize we had gained a combined weight of almost forty pounds).

The second wave was floral—very traditional. My wife loved that our house looked and smelled beautiful, but I thought it looked and smelled like a funeral home. I will never forget one arrangement, from a dear friend. The florist had the inspired idea of putting it in a "treasure chest." I was a bit taken aback when I opened my door to see a delivery man holding a dark wood box, fourteen by eight inches, with a rounded top flipped open to display orchids and lilies. *Really?* I wondered. *A baby casket?* I thought I was being paranoid. But out of caution, I hid it in the kitchen, barely visible behind other arrangements. My wife walked downstairs, passed the kitchen, and stopped suddenly to ask, "Is that a baby casket?" For the first time in ten days, we laughed.

The third wave of consolation came from friends who wanted to touch base, see if we needed anything. These offers were well intentioned and tiring. They required a response when neither of us had much strength. But sometimes we'd read a message, something like: "We don't know what to say. We love you. We're here." And that was perfect.

We eventually started to respond to e-mails and calls and venture outside where we encountered the fourth wave, the most infuriating. It was the unsolicited mention of "God's plan." I don't know if this evoked rage or was the random place where my rage happened to fall, but when I'd hear someone say, "God's plan," I would immediately think, *Asshole.*

My wife wasn't bothered by it. She'd explain that the concept of God's plan—or its less Catholic/Christian version, "Everything happens for a reason"—brings people comfort, which is what they are trying to provide. To me, it suggests there's an explanation for your pain but you don't get to know it. It's brutal. A person can get headaches and lose sleep trying to remember the actor whose voice is in an animated movie or the name of the woman who slept with Gary Hart (don't Google; it's Donna Rice). So imagine the suffering affixed to the unanswered question of "Why did this happen?"

On my worst days, I would remind myself that in the grander scheme, I was quite lucky. I had a beautiful wife, a lovely home, a good job, a great dog, and solid friends. I also had the freedom to take a two-month leave from the office, and though I knew this was a tremendous luxury, it was also necessary. A psychiatrist had written the accurate yet unsettling words that, in her opinion, I was "not prepared to return to work and won't be for some time."

The doctor was right. My thoughts weren't clear. I had three fender benders in a week. I wasn't sleeping well. I was having memories (that, I expected). And visions (not expected). Too many times I recalled the images and textures I saw and felt that night in the bathroom. A few times I dreamed I was rocking a newborn baby swaddled in a red blanket—just that image. Once I woke in the night and walked around the house. I stopped climbing the stairs back to my bedroom to sit and, for about two minutes, speak to a two-year-old girl with black bangs. I was cognizant enough to know she wasn't a ghost or anything supernatural but rather my mind's way of burning off steam. I told her I was so sorry that I couldn't protect her. She said that she forgave me, and I went back to bed.

Another night, hours after taking a sleeping pill, I woke to use the bathroom, only to walk quickly into a wall and fall backward. On more than one occasion I slept for seventeen hours straight. The doctor said that was normal.

My wife and I tried to make love, but, in her words, it was the "scene of the crime."

A shrink suggested I ask a friend to drag me out of the house on a regular basis. We surfed the chilling waters of Zuma or Venice and I'd talk incessantly (to him, the seals, anything that seemed to listen) about how much it hurt. I was a broken record. Yet he continued to regularly invite me out. Compassion breeds an amazing amount of tolerance.

My brother flew across the country for a night. I felt several seconds behind in every conversation. I went downstairs pretending to get a bottle of wine but was really trying to collect myself, and my brother found me there. I apologized for being slow, and then began to cry. Hard. Uncontrollably. My baby brother held me up, supporting me completely, squeezing me as hard as he could, telling me it was okay. He meant the crying.

A month after the loss, I remembered each hushed back-story or confession of every male I knew who had experienced something similar, and I called them. A colleague whose wife had delivered a stillborn child offered to hang out and have a drink. A friend admitted that he felt embarrassed telling a female coworker that he didn't want to attend a baby shower. Another, who lost his son in the thirty-fifth week, told me that they'd changed apartments to escape the baby's room they had created. He said he took no time off from work—not a single day—yet still didn't understand why he'd misplace things or get lost in midsentence. After a pause, he asked me to keep a secret and said they were pregnant again but too frightened to tell anyone.

My wife and I started taking some short trips, little adventures to get our lives back in motion. A short time later, her period arrived. It was as if her body was saying, "Hey, let's move on."

And we are. It's been almost ten months. Time helped. We are working. We've lost the weight and are making love.

In a parallel universe, I'm changing diapers and craving sleep, but in this one, the adoption process is under way, so somewhere there is, or is about to be, a child who will find his or her way to us, and we will all catch and protect each other. In due time, I'll rock back and forth, holding a swaddled child. In a whirlwind of joy, embarrassment, and hypocrisy, I may even shamelessly think that everything happens for a reason.

And Baby Makes Four

For me, as soon as we started the adoption process, it felt as if a weight had been lifted. Yes, there was a short period (Year Five) when I had had a nervous breakdown, but aside from that, I took comfort in the fact that it was no longer my job to produce the baby.

I felt like that woman in the television ad from the '70s who wore a cocktail dress and held a glass of champagne and announced, "I'm cleaning my bathroom bowl!"

I'd be at work, or in a spin class, or at a party drinking alcohol and eating sushi, and I'd think: *I'm having a baby.*

It seemed just as revolutionary as a time-release toilet-bowl cleanser that someone, somewhere, at that very moment, might be carrying—or conceiving—our baby.

I gleefully threw out my pregnancy tests and the syringes we'd collected that made our closet look as if we were running a needle exchange. My period would come and go without fanfare or tears. We could have sex any time of the month, and I didn't have to prop up my pelvis on a pillow for fifteen minutes afterward. I could actually forget about trying to get pregnant, until someone would say, "That's when you get pregnant, when you stop trying!"

There is nothing worse than being told that the one thing you haven't tried is *not trying*. We did get pregnant once not trying, on our honeymoon, and it was all downhill from there. Soon we realized we needed assistance to have a baby: drugs, science, maybe someone else's eggs, maybe someone else's uterus . . . finally it became clear that what we needed was someone else's baby.

And here's the great thing about adoption: there *are* babies. There are babies in need of homes, and homes in need of babies. It all makes perfect, wonderful sense, and yet friends and family and even strangers feel compelled to tell you about all of the people they know who got pregnant as soon as they started to pursue adoption. "That's what always happens," they say, smiling and nodding encouragingly.

"Well, that's not going to happen to *me*," I would say with finality, but the conversation invariably continued: "That's what my sister-in-law's friend thought, and then she got pregnant with twins!"

I'm telling you, these people are relentless.

Here's one reason why I knew that that was not going to happen to me: I just referenced a commercial from the '70s. And you can't find that commercial on YouTube. I have a *memory* of it. (That's what people had before YouTube.) And the fact that I remember life before YouTube is another indication that I won't get pregnant just because I'm not thinking about it.

And now, thanks to these yea-sayers, I *was* thinking about it, so I definitely wouldn't be getting pregnant. And I didn't want to get pregnant. I wanted to adopt! That's how this conversation started!

That's the other annoying part of the urban myth: that once you try to adopt, you will get pregnant. It implies that by adopting, you are settling.

Maybe at one time Ian and I thought it was important that a baby be biologically ours, but once we started looking critically at egg donors and birth parents, it became abundantly clear that we would have rejected ourselves. We would have taken one look at our age, weight, alcohol and drug consumption, family relationship, and health histories and agreed that these were not the kind of people we'd choose to create our baby.

So no, we were not secretly hoping to get pregnant. We'd let go of that hope, and now we had a new hope. Or a new plan, which is better than a hope. Fuck hope.

Hope was the most complicated relationship I had had during this baby quest. I had tried for so long during the IVF process to hang on to hope, to harness the power of positive thinking. Then I began to wonder if hope had been making the disappointments feel too acute. So I tried lowering my expectations, being less hopeful. And when that didn't work (it even felt like the reason things weren't working) I let go of hope altogether (see Year Five), and as it turns out, hope is like oxygen. You need it to stay alive.

But hope has nothing to do with whether or not you are able to birth a child.

I have two female friends who demonstrated this (so it must be true). They were both trying to get pregnant when I was trying, going through the same IVF hell. One remained optimistic throughout, the other pessimistic. They both felt equally heartbroken when things went wrong, and equally lucky when things finally went right. So together, we decided hope has no role in the miracle of childbirth.

In fact, a "miracle" might be exactly what it is, and despite all of the scientific and biological breakthroughs in fertility, we're not in control of miracles. I don't know who is (because the Octomom confused the issue for me), but I know I'm not.

The Octomom will forever be tied to our baby quest in my mind because she was making news when we were unable to make babies. She gave me a whole new appreciation for the movie *Raising Arizona*, which I loved already, but I could now see how a couple without a child might get annoyed (to the point of criminal activity) with someone who seems to have children to spare. I am not sure what upset me more: the fact that the Octomom had fourteen kids, the fact that she began to do porn to support them, or the fact that, after birthing fourteen children, she still had a body for porn.

Despite the seemingly unfair nature of nature, Ian and I were excited about our decision to adopt, and eager to focus on the business at hand, which *was* like a business, because apparently we had to market ourselves as parents.

Even though there are babies in need of homes and homes

in need of babies, it felt as if we were the sellers and the birth mothers were the buyers, as evidenced by the fact that we needed several homemade Books of Us with photos and hand-written captions explaining how lovely and child-friendly we were, a stash of "thank you for possibly giving us your baby" notes, a lengthy home study that involved four visits from a social worker, the addresses of everywhere we'd ever lived, Red Cross certification, baby proofing, and fingerprinting.

I think the most humiliating part of the process was when I went to a liquor store that offered fingerprinting services, and the middle-aged Asian man inking my thumb asked if I was ready to be a parent. "It's a big job," he said.

Really? Did I need his approval, too? The guy at the liquor store?

There were so many gatekeepers on our adoption journey— social workers, lawyers, and now this guy? And then, of course, there were the birth mothers.

Our lawyer would call with basic information about prospective candidates ("She lives in Texas, she's due in two months, the birth father and sex of the baby are unknown"), and then I would drop whatever I was doing and call right away. It was like calling a radio station for concert tickets— usually the line was busy—which is why you have to call right away, especially in Los Angeles, because the gays are very on top of this stuff.

Our lawyer told us some birth mothers prefer a gay male couple, because then they won't feel replaced as the mother. Still, there are plenty of birth mothers who will accept only a "traditional" (read: heterosexual) home for their baby. That might have been good news if it weren't offensive. Ian didn't think we should take a child from a birth mother who had negative feelings about gay couples, but we had to remind ourselves that the baby would be born with no prejudice, and we would try to raise the child to love everyone equally, and, PS, a lot of these birth mothers were antiabortion, something we also had an issue with since we were pro-choice, but their position might be the reason we were getting a child, so we decided to put our politics aside.

Of course, our friends' and families' politics seemed to bubble up all around us. People felt very comfortable sharing their thoughts about what ethnicity our baby should be, open adoption versus closed, from the United States or abroad . . . it was like we were buying a car; everybody had an opinion.

And some opinions were persuasive. There had been a terrible earthquake in Haiti—maybe you should adopt from Haiti. There were foster children who had been in the system for years; weren't they more deserving?

It was hard enough completing our family, and now we had to decide who was most deserving? Maybe *we* were most deserving. We'd waited five fucking years.

Ian and I finally realized/admitted/confessed/apologized that we wanted to adopt domestically so that we could have a newborn. I was waiting for my father's politically incorrect sigh of relief that we weren't adopting from Africa as Ian had originally wanted to do, but he surprised me by bringing up an entirely new issue—he wanted us to look into Jewish adoption agencies.

Really?

The religion of our unborn child was something I hadn't even considered worrying about. I found myself wanting to adopt whatever child would be most upsetting to my father, but again, there is no place for politics, even if they are only family politics, in adoption.

The important thing, I thought, was that Ian and I had finally made a decision that would allow us to move forward. Until we realized it wasn't our decision. It was the birth mother's. She had to choose us. Which meant she had to be open to two forty-something Jews with a dog who looked as if he could eat a baby for breakfast.

And that is how I came to be pitching myself to pregnant young women in the Midwest. Our lawyer said that I should make the initial call, because a lot of these women have trust issues with men. Understandable, since it's a safe bet a man got them into this predicament.

I would have to phone a complete stranger (who was just as nervous about the call as I was) and try to strike up a natural-sounding conversation that would ideally end with me saying, "Can I send you some pictures?" And then I would send one of our handmade scrapbooks and a cover letter and a personalized note in the hopes that she might decide to give us *a child*, and then invariably we would not hear back.

One situation seemed promising. The birth mother was having twins (something Ian and I discussed and actually got enthusiastic about), but it turned out she was going to jail (something we were less enthusiastic about), and then she rejected us.

And we had great letters of recommendation.

That was one of the more gratifying parts of the adoption process. We got to read letters our friends wrote about why we would make great parents. It was nice to be reminded by our true friends why we were doing this. Of course, most people don't need a letter of recommendation to become parents. The Octomom, for example.

Eventually we talked to a birth mother who was having one child (not two, or eight), and we liked her enough to want to meet her, and miraculously she wanted to meet us, too.

She was seven months pregnant when I first spoke to her. I liked that she seemed not just intelligent, but emotionally intelligent. If we were going to have an open adoption (which we wanted), that seemed important, now and in the future.

When we met her in person in Los Angeles, one month before the baby was due, our nursery was only partially finished.

She confessed later that this worried her. She thought we weren't ready.

If only she knew how ready we were, but Ian had been nervous about another plan collapsing, leaving us with the reminder of an empty nursery. I, on the other hand, wanted to allow myself a little joy; I wanted to behave like a woman who was expecting a baby, thus the compromise of the half-finished nursery. I remember Tink watching, concerned, as the stuff of my home/office went to storage unit R3176, and the paint went up, and the rug went down, and the crib and changing table arrived.

Then the baby arrived.

We even got to be in the delivery room.

I always envisioned being in the delivery room as the person delivering, but instead I was standing by, like the father at a birth, with the father at the birth, Ian.

And as we held hands, and witnessed the miracle of our baby being born, we fell in love all over again. Not just with the baby—a perfect baby girl—but with each other.

And maybe even with the universe.

I have never felt so grateful, so aware of what a gift I was getting, than when this veritable stranger gave us the gift of a baby.

And when we got home with this long-awaited little one, even Tink fell in love.

So now it's the four of us against the world.

But Tink still secretly thinks of the baby as a houseguest.

Welcome to the World

I can't believe it's already been seven years since the FBI knocked on my neighbors' doors to see if anyone knew anything about the man I had just married, Ian Wallach.

That's how I met my next-door neighbor, Karla, the first in a long line of L.A. neighbors I would meet thanks to Ian.

In all of my years living at the beach pre-Ian, I'd never so much as introduced myself to Karla. And still, she was kind enough to stop by and let me know that an FBI agent had been at her house, and at a number of houses on the block, asking questions about Ian, and the agent would not, or could not, disclose why he was asking.

She smiled gingerly, as if this might be the first I was hearing that I had married a fugitive. For all she knew, Ian was a drug lord, or serial killer, or both. She and the other neighbors were concerned for me. And, I imagine, for the neighborhood.

I was concerned, too. I had a lot of unanswered questions, such as:

Where had the FBI been for my previous relationships? Why

had I had to figure out *on my own* if those were good guys or bad guys? Why now, when the wedding had already happened, when the photo album had been finalized, when the gift receipts had been tossed, were my tax dollars finally at work helping me figure out what sort of person I was sleeping with?

Here's why:

Ian, after leaving his job at a big law firm in New York, was doing pro bono work through the Center for Constitutional Rights representing Guantanamo Bay detainees, and his access to classified documents necessitated FBI clearance.

Neither Ian nor I had realized that clearance would include door-to-door questioning, but that's how my neighbors, who barely knew me, found out that I had gotten married. Not by invitation—by interrogation.

In the years to come, Ian—and then Ian and Tink—would meet almost all of my neighbors, and definitely all of their dogs. Ian would tell me who we should invite to our house for a four-ingredient meal (everyone), who was moving, who was pregnant, who was dying, who needed cheering up, and who needed avoiding.

Upon hearing his news, I would always say, "Who are you talking about? A dog or a person?" (Tinkerbell might be a dumb name for a dog, but at least it's clear she's a pet. Shaun, Jessie, Oscar, Leyla—I wasn't sure if they were puppies or children, afflicted with fleas or the flu.)

But one thing was clear. I would never be anonymous again. I was now "the other person who owns Tinkerbell," or less generously, "the unfriendly wife of Ian Wallach."

At least, I felt like that's how I was known. Ian would always encourage me to come with him on his dog-walking rounds, but I wasn't ready to let the world in. I was still getting used to letting Ian in, not to mention Tink. Who needed neighbors?

And then came our daughter.

Olivia.

She was the tipping point.

Once you have a baby, you become a citizen of the world whether you like it or not, and nobody was more surprised than I was to realize I liked my new status. I liked being part of a community. And I really liked being a mother.

It probably sounds crazy and ungrateful, after so many years of trying, to be *surprised* that I liked being a mother, but I think that it was precisely because we'd been trying for so long that I had simply stopped imagining life with a child. I had stopped imagining a future in general after so many disappointments, so now that we had finally adopted a baby, I was learning to allow myself to enjoy her.

Even the sleepless nights everybody warned us about weren't so bad. Maybe because my body didn't go through the trauma of childbirth, maybe because we'd waited so long to hear a baby cry—when Olivia would wake crying for a bottle, Ian and I were both kind of excited to be the one to give it to her.

Ian doesn't remember it that way. He says I would invent "ghost feedings" by telling him I was up at three and that it was his turn now . . . when actually it was the night before that I had been up at three. It all became a blur, but we both remember being awake in those late hours, and being tired but happy.

Karla (after I found out she was my next-door neighbor) sold her house to a couple who was expecting a baby girl two weeks after we adopted Olivia, and they have become the kind of neighbors I never dreamed existed—the kind you are hoping will stop by, the kind who bring leftover brownies, the kind who are great friends to you and your daughter. Olivia and their daughter Eva are like sisters. They have literally been best friends their whole lives. And Olivia always says, "Night night, Eva" to their house as we walk upstairs to her bedroom.

She also says "night night" to the other kids in the neighborhood—Dorian, Max, Violet, Little Violet, Benny, Harlie, Devan, the girl from her music class. . . .

And I know these kids. And I know their nannies and parents and even their dogs.

And here's the weird thing. I like knowing them.

Now when Ian and I go to the farmers' market on Sunday, several of Olivia's friends will be there, and I'm not annoyed to run into them or their parents.

I never realized what a curmudgeon I was! I'm not sure why I was always in such a rush to avoid people, but I'm not anymore.

I think my friend Winnie Holzman said it best when she told me, after I had Olivia, "Isn't it great having a baby? Doesn't it make you a better person?" She went on to explain her theory that not everyone needs a baby to become a better person, that some people can become better people on their own, but she needed a baby to do it.

And I think I did, too.

A husband can only force you so far out of your comfort zone (and Ian gives it his best shot, every day), but a baby catapults you into a world so foreign, a place so new, you have no choice but to seek help from your spouse, your parents, your friends, strangers, anyone who has information, even if it's bad information.

You have no choice but to become a citizen of the world.

For me, that meant that all of the babies I had ignored for so many years, stepped around, wished quiet—now they were little people with big personalities and sippy cup preferences. And their parents were tired people with nap schedules and Cheerios in their pockets. And everyone suddenly seemed so connected and relevant to me that I could no longer ignore the rest of the world, nor did I want to.

And it's not just babies and parents. I now stop people with dogs to ask how old their dog is. That is something Ian used to do, and I always thought, *Who cares? Why are we stopping?* But I now understand, as a fellow dog owner, that when a stranger assumes your dog is younger than your dog really is, it makes you extremely happy. It's as good—or better— than being told *you* look young, because being told your dog looks young means maybe you have longer with your dog. I see this now. I see the dog, and then I see the owner, just like now I see the child, and then I see the parent. I never used to see any of this.

I still see single women, of course. I've always seen them. I still relate and sympathize with their plight—the checking of the text messages, the debating of the scone, the making of the small talk on a bad date. Having been a single woman myself for so many years, and knowing I could be one again at any moment (this is Los Angeles, after all), I hope this book is an optimistic reminder that the happy ending of marriage is not an ending. It's another beginning.

And I now see married women. I especially feel for married women, because it's so hard to talk about your problems without feeling disloyal, or worrying you're opening a door you will never be able to shut again. Not everyone is willing to spill every sordid detail about her marriage in a book, especially while she is still in the marriage and hoping to stay in the marriage.

Initially Ian worried that a book like this was inviting an ironic end. He told me that if I wrote a book about how great we were together, we would certainly break up and look very foolish, to which I replied, "Don't worry. It's not about how great we are together."

But I can't help feeling that Olivia is the happy ending to this chapter of my life, even though I know she is the beginning of another.

I am a parent.

I was never in this club before. I knew it existed, but the line was always so long, I didn't bother looking inside. And now I live inside the club, and it's a crazy place with crazy hours, and I'm so happy—as Ian put it, since we both live life fully—that we are not missing this big part of life.

I hate saying that, because I was so comforted knowing we didn't *have* to have a child. And we could have had a nice life without one, I'm sure. But it wouldn't have been *this* life.

I realized I had crossed over to the other side when I caught myself showing baby pictures that nobody asked to see. I was never someone who oohed and aahed over baby pictures. If you don't have a baby, it seems strange that you have to see a picture every time you see a friend with a child. *Didn't I see one last time?* I used to think.

But now I'm the one showing pictures, because Olivia is so much better than anything Ian and I could have created on our own, and I just have to show her off.

I do feel, though, as if we're helping create her every day, when Ian takes her up to the roof to light a magic balloon (like the one we wished on in Thailand) and almost sets the neighborhood on fire. Or when we take her traveling with us and we are suddenly the people I used to hate on planes, except that now I can't tell who is more annoying—Olivia for crying, or Ian for singing and making funny noises until she stops. Or when I read to her and she "reads" to me, and we laugh about things she's learned from reading, like the fact that she's become the pigeon who wants to stay up late.

She has a little of both of us in her, and a little something magical that nobody can take credit for, which I now know is the case with all children, no matter how they came into this world.

One night recently, I was putting Olivia to bed, and even though we've had two years to get used to it, Ian and I still both love being the person who gets to put her to bed. I'm not sure if this is because we're still amazed we finally have a baby, or if we're just sick of each other, but each night one of us takes a turn being the parent who sits in the big over-stuffed chair in Olivia's room to read her a bedtime story while twinkly stars dance on the ceiling (because, of course, Ian had to order a planetarium projector from Japan).

And on this particular night, I was too lazy, or just too cozy sitting with Olivia, to get out of the overstuffed chair and get a book from the shelf, so I decided to make up a story instead.

That's what I do for a living. How hard could it be?

The backstory of this bedtime tale is that when Olivia was a newborn, anytime she was sleeping soundly, it was Ian who was the stereotypical worried parent, convinced she wasn't breathing. He would put his hand in front of her mouth until he could feel her breath, or he would wake me to wake her. I always felt that he was being slightly ridiculous. I knew she was okay. I don't know why I was so confident, but one of the few things I did *not* worry about was whether Olivia was breathing when she slept. She seemed quite capable on her own. It was the two of us, the adults in the house, who were in constant need of manuals and reassurance.

But one night when I got home late from work, I did what you're not supposed to do as a parent: I picked up a sleeping baby and held her in my arms and rocked her for few minutes, not because she needed it, but because I did.

And during those few minutes, there was an earthquake.

Now, in California, you have a lot of earthquakes, and this was not a large one. Olivia didn't even wake up, but still I was so relieved that I was holding her at that moment that I didn't have to worry about getting to her to protect her.

And I started thinking about what I would do if anything ever happened to her, and if I couldn't get to her, or if I could get to her, but still couldn't help her, and it took my breath away. I finally knew how Ian felt all of those nights, how all parents feel at some point—that you would not be able to go on if anything ever happened to your child.

And then I thought: *My mother, Ian's mother—they can't still feel this way, because that would be untenable! It would be impossible to go through life feeling this much love and worry all of the time! Clearly at some point, maybe when the child rebels, the parent can also step back. It must be like a breakup,* I thought; *both people don't necessarily want it, but you have no choice—you have to move on when the other person does.*

I asked my mom and Ian's mom if this was the case—if there was a point, as mothers, when they felt that they could finally exhale.

And they both told me the horrible truth: you never love your child any less, or worry about your child any less.

Oh. My. God.

I suddenly regretted every time I've ever worried my mother. Or said something hurtful. Or just not called.

And I regretted reading the *hilarious* story of Ian's apartment rappelling incident to his mother, who did not find the story funny. At the time, I thought she just didn't get it.

Oh, she got it, all right. And even though Ian was clearly fine, had lived to tell the tale, and was laughing along with me as I told the story, there was a moment (when I explained how Ian might have fallen to his death) that his mother was more horrified than amused.

She explained that, as a mother, you not only continue to feel what I was feeling for Olivia, it grows.

It *grows*?! How could this love grow? I could barely contain it already.

I felt sick. And that's what I was thinking about when I started to tell Olivia a bedtime story.

I told her that our love for her was like a giant hot-air balloon, and the more we loved her, the higher we went. And every day we loved her more, so every day, we went higher and higher, past the trees, past the birds, through the clouds. And then at some point . . . we realized we were too high. We had to get back down. But how?

How indeed? I had no fucking idea!

Why had I started this story (the one I was telling, not to mention the one I was living!) if I didn't know how to get to a safe, happy ending?

I still don't know how people get down from this height.

And, of course, I am very appreciative that Ian is in this

balloon with me, but let's be honest: he is no help. His love for me and Olivia is just making the problem worse. He is taking us higher than I ever wanted to go.

And as I thought about this, how Ian's love was making things worse, I had an idea for an ending—if not for life, then for Olivia's story.

I told her that in order to land, we would have to love everything else in the world as well. We would have to love all of the other children, and the birds and the trees and the earth and the animals and the people, even the weird people, and eventually everything else would float up or we would float down—I wasn't sure about the specific mechanics of it—but I assured her that by loving everything else in the world in addition to one another, we wouldn't feel so vulnerable and alone. (Or, at least, I wouldn't.)

"So," I continued, "we loved the animals and the trees and the people, and eventually, we got back down and crawled out of the balloon and went to sleep."

I looked at Olivia to see if I stuck the landing, so to speak, and I guess I did, because she was asleep, just like in the story.

I felt kind of proud of myself.

I also felt like I could exhale for what seemed like the first time since the earthquake, which had actually taken place several months earlier.

So, maybe taking a chance on loving someone and committing your life to that person (even if that person is sometimes crazy), and then taking a chance on creating a family (even if it is very hard to create, even if the pain and loss are sometimes too much to bear), maybe all of that gives you the chance to see higher highs than you ever imagined.

Which, of course, means you have farther to fall.

The altitude still scares me.

I feel like there is so much to lose.

I feel, quite often, like life was easier when it was just me, just one person, safely grounded, but it's too late for that.

We're already in the balloon—all of us—not just me, but Ian, Olivia, even Tink (who is not comfortable with this situation either, as evidenced by her need for all of us to be in one room whenever possible). We're all in this thing—the neighborhood, our families, our friends, our dogs and cats, and you . . . you people just falling in love, just moving in together, just getting married, just having a baby, just reading this sentence. . . .

We're all in this together.

Acknowledgments

Mostly I have to thank Ian, who could not have been a better sport as I was writing this book and as we were living these chapters. The fact that no matter what I wrote, he still came off as dreamy . . . well, that just proves how limited I am as a writer, and how dreamy Ian is as a human being.

I want to thank my mom for being such a warm and wonderful mother, and also for giving me Grandma Ruby's bentwood rocking chair, which spent a lot of time in storage unit R3176 before making the transition back to the Fabulous Beach House (aka the House of Sand and Fur). I remember my mother and grandmother rocking me in it, and now Olivia's favorite thing is to rock in it herself until it knocks into a wall.

I want to thank my dad, who calls some parts of this book "the bad parts," meaning there is too much information for a dad, and maybe for an audience. So if you were ever uncomfortable reading something, you have my dad to thank for trying to shield you, for telling me that some things might be too personal, that not everyone needs to know everything. As usual, I didn't listen to him, and now, karmically, I have a daughter who will not listen to me someday, and I can only hope I live to see it.

I want to thank the storytelling community of Los Angeles, which supported and encouraged me as I read many of these chapters in progress. I will always have a soft spot in my heart for live storytelling and spoken word events, not only because they brought me and Ian together, but also because they remind everyone lucky enough to be listening how compelling, hilarious, poignant, and healing a true story can be.

I want to thank my literary agent, Joy Harris, because she told me many years ago that I should write a book about marriage, which is why I wanted her to represent me. I had not planned to write a book about marriage—I was still wondering what I had to say on the subject—but she was sure I would have plenty to say, and apparently she was right.

I want to thank my editor at Viking, Rick Kot. From the beginning he made me feel that I had a story worth telling, and at times when I worried nobody would care about me or my marriage or my dog, he assured me that at the very least, people would care about the dog. (I'm kidding, although it's true that he's a dog person, which I now love in a person, but also, he is a book person, and a friend to writers, and I feel very lucky to have had him on board even before there was a baby on board.)

Speaking of which, I want to thank—and apologize to— Olivia. This is probably more than you wanted to know, and yet I hope you grow up loving your story, and seeing the humor and heartache in everyone and everything. I am so happy you came into my life (and my book). Your father and I could not love you more.

But we will. Every day. For the rest of our lives. And then some.

Publication Notes

"Get This":
   Published in Dutton's *Girls Who Like Boys Who Like Boys* anthology, May 2008; shorter version published in *New York Times* "Modern Love" column, May 6, 2007.

"Oh, How We Love Bad Boys":
   Published in *People's Sexiest Man Alive* issue, November 28, 2005; included in the St. Martin's Press *What Was I Thinking?* anthology.

"In Sickness and in Health":
   Written for the Stand Up to Cancer Web site, posted May 2008; Published in *O, The Oprah Magazine*'s October 2008 issue.

"The First No No Noel":
   Published in the *New York Times* Sunday "Styles" section, December 24, 2006.

"Now We're Cooking?":
   Published in *O, The Oprah Magazine*'s April 2008 issue.

"We're Having a Maybe!":
   Published in the St. Martin's Press *Afterbirth* anthology, April

2009; shorter version published in O, *The Oprah Magazine*'s September 2008 issue.

"Eggspecting":
(Note from Cindy: I wrote "Eggspecting" in July 2009 and it was slated to appear in the *New York Times* "Modern Love" column, but then we lost the baby, so I pulled the piece because, as you can see, that's not something easily put into a footnote.)

"A Father's Story: The Baby We Never Had," by Ian Wallach:
Published in O, *The Oprah Magazine*'s October 2010 issue.